Best Easy Day Hikes
Grand Staircase-Escalante and the
Glen Canyon Region

Help Us Keep This Guide Up to Date

Every effort has been made by the authors and editors to make this guide as accurate and useful as possible. However, many things can change after a guide is published—trails are rerouted, regulations change, facilities come under new management, and so forth.

We welcome your comments concerning your experiences with this guide and how you feel it could be improved and kept up to date. While we may not be able to respond to all comments and suggestions, we'll take them to heart, and we'll also make certain to share them with the authors. Please send your comments and suggestions to the following address:

Globe Pequot Press
Reader Response/Editorial Department
246 Goose Lane
Guilford, CT 06437

Or you may e-mail us at:

editorial@falcon.com

Thanks for your input, and happy trails!

Best Easy Day Hikes Series

Best Easy Day Hikes Grand Staircase– Escalante and the Glen Canyon Region

Third Edition

Ron Adkison

Updated by JD Tanner and Emily Ressler-Tanner

FALCONGUIDES

GUILFORD, CONNECTICUT

FALCONGUIDES®

An imprint of Globe Pequot
Falcon and FalconGuides are registered trademarks and Make Adventure
Your Story is a trademark of Rowman & Littlefield.

Distributed by NATIONAL BOOK NETWORK

Copyright © 2018 Rowman & Littlefield
A previous edition of this book was published by Falcon Publishing,
Inc., in 1998.

TOPO! Maps copyright © 2018 National Geographic Partners, LLC. All
Rights Reserved.
Maps © Rowman & Littlefield

British Library Cataloguing-in-Publication Information available

Library of Congress Cataloging-in-Publication Data available

ISBN 978-1-4930-2885-6 (paperback)
ISBN 978-1-4930-2886-3 (e-book)

∞ ™ The paper used in this publication meets the minimum requirements
of American National Standard for Information Sciences—Permanence
of Paper for Printed Library Materials, ANSI/NISO Z39.48-1992.

Printed in the United States of America

Contents

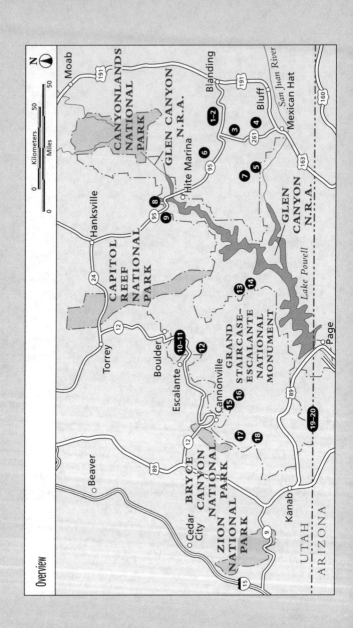

About the Authors 128

Introduction

The relatively undiscovered Glen Canyon region, stretching from Cedar Mesa near Blanding, Utah, to the Paria River Canyon near Glen Canyon Dam on the Arizona–Utah border, features hundreds of miles of excellent hiking and canyoneering routes in southern Utah. Within this region, hikers can enjoy outstanding canyon-country landscapes with scenery rivaling that found in Utah's well-known national parks, but without the hordes of hikers that flock to those famous areas.

This handy guidebook, an abridged version of the comprehensive book *Hiking Grand Staircase–Escalante and the Glen Canyon Region*, is the first book about the Glen Canyon region that meets the needs of day hikers, whether they are a family on vacation or more serious hikers budgeting their time and energy.

The twenty easy hikes in this book survey the spectrum of the Glen Canyon region's landscapes: serpentine canyons and wooded plateaus, arches, natural bridges, Anasazi ruins, and rock art sites. The hikes range from less than a mile to 8 miles, although most are 2 to 3 miles in length. A few of the hikes have steep or sustained grades, though most are gentle with minimal elevation change. Many of the hikes covered in this book are on well-defined, easy-to-follow trails. Only a few are trail less, and those routes follow canyon-bottom washes where route-finding skills are not necessary.

Weather

Hikers come to the Glen Canyon region year-round, but most visit during spring and autumn. Since the region is a desert environment, with daytime high temperatures often reaching 95 to 105 degrees Fahrenheit, June through August, summer is the most unfavorable time of the year to hike in the area.

Spring weather (March through May) can be highly variable, with daytime high temperatures ranging from the 50s to the 70s and nighttime lows ranging from 20 to 50 degrees Fahrenheit. Occasional cold fronts from the west and northwest can bring cold and windy conditions, rain showers in the lower elevations, and perhaps snow on the higher mesas. Generally warm, dry weather prevails between storm systems.

The onset of searing summer heat usually begins in late May and can persist into mid-September. The monsoon season usually begins in mid-July and ends in mid-September. During this time, moist tropical air masses over Mexico circulate an almost daily parade of thunderstorms over the region. Midsummer weather in southern Utah is characterized by torrential rainfall, which is usually accompanied by strong, gusty winds and lightning.

Autumn provides some of the most stable weather of the year. Clear, warm, sunny days and cool nights make this one of the most delightful seasons to visit the Glen Canyon region. Expect daytime highs to range from the 70s and 80s in September to the 40s and 50s by November. Overnight lows are typically in the 20- to 50-degree range. Cold fronts can sweep through the region as autumn progresses, and by mid- to late October in some years, these fronts can drop temperatures significantly for several days or longer. Snowfall in the higher elevations is not uncommon.

Winter in the Glen Canyon region is cold and often windy, and deep snow sometimes covers the ground above

6,000 feet. Cold-weather experience is essential for winter hiking in the region.

Safety and Preparations

All of the areas covered in this book are in wild, very remote country, far removed from enclaves of civilization. You must come prepared to be self-reliant, with a good attitude and ample supplies to deal with unexpected situations.

Hikers should note that hiking in canyon country is more demanding than they might expect. Sandy washes and trails, cairned routes over slickrock, navigating among boulders, rock-hopping, and forging a way through streamside growth go with the territory. Hikers new to canyon-country hiking should take it slow and be careful until they grow accustomed to the rigors of travel here.

All hikers should carry at least two quarts of water per person on half-day hikes and one gallon per person on all-day hikes in hot weather. Avoid hiking in the Glen Canyon region during the hot summer months, but if you must, walk during the early morning and late afternoon hours only.

Always tell someone back home where you will be each day, and in the event you do not contact that person at the end of your trip as planned, make arrangements for him or her to notify the county sheriff in your area of travel. Sheriffs' phone numbers are listed for each chapter.

Be aware that road and hiking conditions can change rapidly. Always obtain updated information on your route of travel from the Bureau of Land Management (BLM) offices listed in each chapter. Flash floods can occur suddenly, leaving you stranded in canyons or on rain-slick dirt roads. Always be prepared with extra food, water, and clothing in

the event you become stranded, whether in the backcountry
or on the road.

Items Every Hiker Should Carry
- At least two quarts of water per person
- First-aid kit (including bandages, moleskin, lip balm, sunscreen)
- Signal mirror
- Food
- Map
- Fleece or parka
- Rain gear or windproof parka
- Hat with brim
- Hiking boots, lightweight and durable
- Toilet paper, trowel, and ziplock bag (for packing out used toilet paper)
- Sunglasses

You are permitted to bring your dog on trails in all areas covered in this book except in Natural Bridges National Monument, Slickhorn Canyon, Grand Gulch down canyon from the mouth of Collins Canyon, and Coyote Gulch. Keep your dog under restraint at all times, and never allow it to foul precious water sources. In Glen Canyon National Recreation Area, you are required to leash your dog. The desert is unforgiving to dogs not accustomed to the hot, dry environment. Carry extra water in dry areas, and offer it to your dog frequently. Hot rocks and sand will quickly burn your dog's paws, and dogs can overheat easily, so avoid bringing your pet in hot weather. Consider outfitting your dog with dog boots. Ruffwear makes an excellent pair, which can be purchased on their website and at many local outfitters.

Cellular phones generally receive a good signal in the region, particularly in areas within sight of Kanab, Utah, and Navajo Mountain. Having a cell phone with you will provide an extra measure of security in the event you run into trouble.

Leave No Trace

The desert landscape of southern Utah appears deceptively durable, but it is very fragile. Once damaged, the desert recovers slowly and may not heal completely in your lifetime, if at all. Soils in this slickrock-dominated canyon country are thin to nonexistent. Plants and desert creatures balance delicately here to survive. The simple act of walking off the trail, even for short distances, can crush plants, move rocks, and otherwise disrupt this balance. Shortcuts and excavation at campsites hasten erosion of the thin soil cover, reducing and, in some instances, eliminating habitat for plants and animals. Shortcutting trails can also lead to the eventual destruction of a good, but perhaps unmaintained, trail.

Most canyon-country hikers have long since learned to employ no-trace practices. Along most of the Glen Canyon region's trails and routes and at its campsites, you will seldom find trash, food scraps, discarded items, soapsuds in precious water sources, evidence of illegal campfires, or unnecessary excavations or alterations. Consider the following ideas for zero-impact travel as guidelines for preserving the wilderness resource, not only for the desert's native inhabitants, but also for those who follow in your footsteps.

Waste
Garbage and food scraps attract animals, ants, and flies. Pack out your garbage and leftover food scraps with the rest of your trash.

Human waste must be deposited at least 200 feet from campsites, trails, water sources, and drainages. Choose a spot with organic soil and dig a cat hole 6 to 8 inches deep, covering the waste with soil. In many areas in the Glen Canyon region, you will be hiking in washes and canyons, so if you are unable to get 200 feet from the water source, please pack out solid human waste. You can get WAG bags and Restops from the land management agencies throughout the region or at local guide shops and gear stores. Both of these products are approved by the Environmental Protection Agency (EPA) for landfills.

Do not bury or burn your toilet paper. Fires from burning toilet paper have devastated parts of the region; areas of Grand Gulch and Paria Canyon are examples. Some areas require you to pack out your used toilet paper, and most experienced canyoneers do, since decomposition is very slow in the desert. Ziplock bags are useful for this.

Stay on the Trail

The passage of too many feet creates a lasting trail in the Utah desert, whether it be from campsite to water source or an off-trail route that can evolve into a trail. Use established trails where they are available. Your boot tracks in trail less areas will encourage others to follow.

Cryptobiotic Soil Crusts

In some areas of the Glen Canyon region, you will find large areas of soil covered by a black or gray lumpy crust. This delicate assemblage of mosses, lichens, blue-green algae, and fungi forms a protective layer against wind and water erosion and aids in the absorption and retention of moisture, allowing larger plants to gain a foothold. The passage of a single hiker can destroy this fragile crust, and it may take twenty-five years or longer to redevelop. In areas covered by cryptobiotic soil crust, it is essential that hikers stick to established trails or follow routes over slickrock or sand.

Archaeological Sites

Evidence of ancient cultures abounds in the Glen Canyon region, particularly on Cedar Mesa. Along some trails and routes, you are very likely to encounter archaeological and historical ruins and artifacts.

The majority of archaeological sites date back to between AD 1050 and 1200 (although evidence suggests occupation of the Cedar Mesa region as early as AD 200), a time when the Anasazi widely occupied the area. Granaries, rock art, ruins of dwellings, potsherds, and chipping sites are among the cultural resources hikers may find in the Glen Canyon backcountry.

Keep in mind that these nonrenewable resources offer archaeologists insight into past ways of life in the region and can be easily disturbed and damaged by curious hikers. Although federal and state laws protect cultural resources, ultimately it depends on each of us to walk softly and treat these resources with the respect they deserve. Excavation and stabilization of many sites has yet to take place. Although hikers are likely to encounter many archaeological sites on trails and routes in the region, this book will not lead you to them, preserving for hikers the sense of discovery.

Ancient granaries and ruins are very fragile. Restrain the urge to enter or climb on their stone walls, and walk carefully around the slopes that support these structures. Ruins are best observed from a distance with the aid of binoculars. That way you will reduce your impact to zero. Areas with ruins are essentially outdoor museums, and visitors should conduct themselves as they would in any museum displaying irreplaceable artifacts. Ruins are an interesting highlight of a hike but are inappropriate places to make camp.

After observing an archaeological site, move on before having meals. Food crumbs and garbage may attract rodents that could then nest in the site.

Skin oils easily destroy pigments of ancient pictographs. Restrain the urge to touch them, particularly handprint pictographs. Never add your own graffiti to irreplaceable rock art panels.

If you happen upon an archaeological site where artifacts remain, you may photograph them, but if you pick up or rearrange objects, you may be destroying an important link to the past. Once an artifact is removed or disturbed, it becomes merely an object with little meaning to archaeologists. And if you observe any unlawful or inappropriate behavior at archaeological sites, report the activity to the nearest BLM office.

Canine Considerations

Regulations in many areas require that your dog be leashed at all times. No one wants to be confronted by a barking or overly friendly dog while in the backcountry. Many dogs can't resist cooling off in precious desert water sources, chasing wildlife, stirring up silt, and fouling the source for the hikers who follow. At archaeological sites, unleashed dogs can cause damage by running and digging in the midden, by jumping over walls, and by climbing into ruins. Steep cliffs, wildlife, and traps are just a few of the hazards your dog may encounter in this area. It is therefore critical that dog owners either leave their dogs at home or keep them leashed and under control at all times while in the backcountry. Dog waste spreads disease, fouls water sources, and is a negative social impact for other users. Dog owners should plan on picking up after their pets and packing out all dog waste.

The Falcon Principles of Zero Impact

- Leave with everything you brought with you.
- Leave no sign of your visit.
- Leave the landscape as you found it.

For more information on minimizing your impact while hiking, please contact the Leave No Trace Center for Outdoor Ethics at (800) 332-4100 or visit their website at LNT.org.

How to Use This Guide

The hike descriptions in this guide provide all the information you need to inform and prepare you for your backcountry trip. Here are a few additional points to help you get the most out of the guide:

The **Distance** heading tells how long, in miles, a hike is. This listing also tells you if the hike is a round-trip, in which you retrace your route to the trailhead after reaching your destination, or a loop trip, in which you hike in on one trail and return to your starting point by another trail.

The **Hiking time** is based on the average hiker. Most hiking times listed are conservative estimates, and many hikers will make the trip in less time. Keep in mind that on many of the region's trails and routes, your pace will average about 1.5 to 2 miles per hour.

The **Difficulty** rating is based on the average hiker's ability and may vary depending on your physical condition and state of mind, as well as the weather and trail or route conditions. This book focuses on shorter, more commonly used trails and routes leading to many of the region's highlights. Difficult canyoneering routes, where advanced rock-climbing skills are required, were omitted.

The **Trail surface** listing tells you if you will be following a constructed trail; a boot-worn trail, where the path has been forged by the passage of other hikers; a cow trail, usually a well-defined path worn by cattle; a well-worn trail, which may be a constructed trail that is no longer maintained but is easy to follow; a wash route, where there is no trail but you follow the path of a canyon's drainage, or wash; a slickrock route, where you follow a trail less way over bare, smooth sandstone (known as slickrock) and where there may be cairns (piles of rocks) to indicate the course of the route; a cross-country route, where there is no established trail and you use basic route-finding skills and landmarks to find the way; or a road or 4WD road, usually a doubletrack that is seldom used by vehicles.

The **Best season** listing indicates the seasons providing the greatest probability of avoiding extreme summer heat and winter snow and cold. Of course, you can hike in most of the Glen Canyon region year-round, but summer and winter hiking present challenges that cannot be taken lightly.

The **Canine compatibility** section lets you know if dogs are permitted on the trail. It also contains warnings about trails that allow dogs, but the terrain is such that bringing your dog would either be dangerous or make travel difficult. Please use your best judgment when considering bringing your dog on any of the hikes in this guide.

Knowing a hike's **Water availability** is critical to a safe and enjoyable trip in the desert environment of the Glen Canyon region. Remember that conditions change constantly in these canyons, and springs can dry up. Always check with the appropriate BLM office for up-to-date information on water availability before heading into the backcountry.

Hazards indicates the dangers of a route such as flash flood danger or steep drop-offs; it also indicates trail less routes that should be avoided by inexperienced hikers if there is a risk of becoming disoriented or lost. One thing that is not described here is the remoteness of a hike, since *all* of these hikes are in very remote areas, where help is far removed should you need it. Always be prepared and self-sufficient.

Permits for backcountry use are required for only a few areas covered in this guide. When necessary, this listing tells where to obtain them and if a fee is required.

Maps indicate additional maps to supplement those found in this book. Hikers wishing to explore further, or off trail, should carry these maps, as they provide much greater detail.

Finding the trailhead provides basic directions to each of the trails included in this book. As many of the trails are in remote locations, a detailed Utah road map will prove a helpful tool in navigating many of the roads in this region.

The hike provides a narrative description of the hiking route and many of the landmarks you will encounter along the way. There are also descriptions of relevant natural and human history.

Miles and directions shows the cumulative mileage between prominent features and junctions. Unnamed features mentioned in the hike descriptions are referred to as "Point 4772" and "Dome 5961."

Maps

The overview map indicates major access roads to each trailhead and, possibly more important, the relative location of hikes to one another to help you plan a whole day or weekend of great hiking in one general vicinity.

The route map is your primary guide to each hike. It shows all accessible roads and trails, points of interest, water, towns, landmarks, and geographical features. It also distinguishes trails from roads and paved roads from unpaved roads. The selected route is highlighted, and directional arrows point the way.

These maps are not intended to replace more detailed agency maps, road maps, state atlases, and topographic maps, but they do indicate the general lay of the trail and its attractions to help you visualize and navigate its course.

For your own purposes, you may wish to copy the directions for a route onto a small sheet to help you while hiking or photocopy the map and the "Miles and Directions" section of a hike to take with you. Otherwise, just slip the whole book in your pack and take it all with you. Enjoy your time in the outdoors, and remember to pack out what you pack in.

A variety of good maps covering the Grand Staircase–Escalante and Glen Canyon regions are useful not only for backcountry navigation but also for navigation on the many remote desert roads accessing trailheads. *Trails Illustrated* topographic maps offer a good overview of two of the three regions covered in this book. For the Cedar Mesa region, use the Grand Gulch Plateau map (706), and for the Escalante region, use the Canyons of the Escalante map (710).

U.S. Geological Survey (USGS) topo maps offer the most detailed representation of the landscape, although they are not a necessity since getting lost while hiking in the bottom of a canyon is unlikely, especially when the wash is the only possible route. Yet for areas not covered by any other maps, such as the Grand Staircase, USGS maps are your only choice. BLM produces a variety of 1:100,000-scale metric maps that will help you navigate through the Glen Canyon region. Hikers en route to and from trailheads in the Grand Staircase region should use the BLM Kanab and Smoky Mountain maps.

If hiking in the Paria Canyon–Vermilion Cliffs Wilderness, either use USGS quadrangles or obtain a copy of the *Hiker's Guide to Paria Canyon*, a BLM publication showing strip maps of all the canyons in the wilderness.

USGS topo maps, BLM maps, and *Trails Illustrated* maps are available at the Kane Gulch Ranger Station (typically open March 1 through June 15 and September 1 through October 31) and Natural Bridges National Monument on Cedar Mesa; at the Escalante Interagency Visitor Center and Escalante Outfitters in Escalante; at the Kanab BLM office and Willow Creek Bookstore in Kanab; and at the Paria Contact Station between Page, Arizona, and Kanab.

You can order the *Utah Road and Recreation Atlas* and USGS quads from the Canyonlands Natural History Association in Moab, Utah; online at cnha.org; or by calling (800) 840-8978. *Trails Illustrated* maps can also be ordered directly from National Geographic Maps by visiting their website at http://www.natgeomaps.com/trail-maps/trails-illustrated-maps/utah or by calling (800) 962-1643.

Books and maps covering the entire Glen Canyon region can be ordered by mail from Escalante Outfitters in Escalante by calling (866) 455-0041. For the Grand Staircase and Paria Canyon, order books and maps by mail from the Willow Canyon Outdoor at willowcanyon.com or by calling (435) 644-8884.

Trail Finder

Best Hikes for Canyons

Best Hikes for Bridges, Arches, and Rock Formations

Best Hikes for Archaeological/Historical Sites and Ruins

Best Hikes for Waterfalls

Map Legend

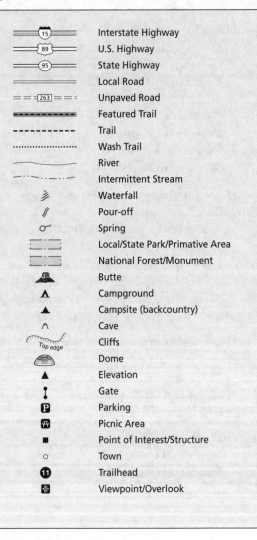

═══════🛡15🛡═══════	Interstate Highway
──────🛡89🛡──────	U.S. Highway
─────🛡95🛡─────	State Highway
───────────────	Local Road
= = =🛡263🛡= = =	Unpaved Road
▬▬▬▬▬▬▬▬▬	Featured Trail
- - - - - - - - -	Trail
· · · · · · · · · · · · ·	Wash Trail
～～～～～	River
─·─··─··─··─	Intermittent Stream
〰	Waterfall
//	Pour-off
o⌐	Spring
▭ ▭ ▭	Local/State Park/Primative Area
▬ ▬ ▬	National Forest/Monument
🏔	Butte
Ⓐ	Campground
▲	Campsite (backcountry)
∩	Cave
Top edge	Cliffs
◠	Dome
▲	Elevation
┃	Gate
🅿	Parking
🛆	Picnic Area
■	Point of Interest/Structure
○	Town
⑪	Trailhead
🇰	Viewpoint/Overlook

Cedar Mesa

Cedar Mesa is a broad, featureless plateau in southeast Utah, stretching north from Monument Valley and the San Juan River to the lofty tableland of Elk Ridge. Utah highways 95, 261, and 276 bisect this platform, where drivers are enveloped in pinyon-juniper woodlands and pass by unaware of the myriad canyons that cleave the mesa's surface.

The canyons of Cedar Mesa offer some of the most outstanding hiking opportunities in the Glen Canyon region, yet most of these gorges are overlooked by hikers en route to more well-known southern Utah destinations. All of the canyons are carved into the mesa's namesake rock formation, the Cedar Mesa sandstone, one of the most notable scenery producers in the canyon country of the Colorado Plateau. This resistant rock forms great bulging cliffs, often overhanging, resulting from the differential erosion of hard and less-resistant beds of red and white sandstone. Hoodoos, spires of resistant rock sculpted by erosion, and mushroom rocks, a type of hoodoo shaped like a mushroom, typically punctuate the rims of the convoluted canyon walls.

Because of the Cedar Mesa sandstone's response to weathering and erosion, great slickrock amphitheaters, cave-like alcoves, and ledges dimple the canyon walls. It is in these hidden niches where people of the Anasazi culture long ago built their homes of rock, sticks, and mortar and stored their grain. Ruins of this ancient culture and its mysterious rock art abound in the Cedar Mesa region, and each canyon here is virtually an outdoor museum of the culture.

Although the Anasazi people left their cliff-bound homes 700 years ago, many of their dwellings and granaries are so well preserved, it seems as if they left last week. An increase in visitation has led to the rapid deterioration of many sites, most often through the inadvertent impact of curious hikers. All visitors are urged to walk softly around these ancient archaeological sites (see the "Leave No Trace" section in this book's introduction).

The nature of the Cedar Mesa sandstone makes most hiking routes in the canyons very demanding and passable only to seasoned canyoneers. Yet there are exceptions, and the trails and routes described below are passable to any hiker. These hikes visit ancient ruins, outstanding lonely canyons, riparian oases, and natural bridges.

Camping

Only one developed campground is located in the Cedar Mesa region, and that is the thirteen-unit campground in Natural Bridges National Monument. This campground is open year-round for a fee and is available on a first-come, first-served basis. It often fills by early afternoon in the spring and autumn, so arrive early if you wish to secure a site.

The campground is set in the pinyon-juniper woodland on the rim of White Canyon and affords fine views into that slickrock gorge and to the lofty prominences of Woodenshoe Buttes and the Bears Ears. Facilities include tables, tent pads, fire grills, and pit toilets. Water is available only at the visitor center, 0.25 mile from the campground.

If the campground is full or your vehicle exceeds 21 feet in length, use the overflow camping area located 6.2 miles east of the visitor center. To get there, drive east of the monument to the UT 95/261 junction and turn right (south) onto

UT 261. About 100 yards south of the junction, signs direct you left (southeast) down a gravel road to the camping area.

Most visitors to the Cedar Mesa region camp at large, or wherever they wish, off the network of San Juan County roads that crisscross the mesa. Here, on public lands administered by the BLM, you will find almost unlimited opportunities to car camp in the pinyon–juniper woodlands. Most sites are short spur roads or pullouts, offering room enough to park and set up a tent. Always use established sites, and never drive off-road and create new sites. Pack out all trash and follow guidelines in this book's "Leave No Trace" section. Extreme caution is advised if you choose to build a campfire.

Access and Services

Access to this remote region is provided by UT 95, a 121-mile highway that links Hanksville in the northwest with Blanding in the southeast, and is unquestionably the most scenic drive in the Colorado Plateau's canyon country. Cedar Mesa can also be reached via UT 261, which branches north from US 191/163, 4 miles north of Mexican Hat, and leads 33 miles to its junction with UT 95.

Services are limited to the communities that lie far beyond Cedar Mesa. Groceries, gas, lodging, car repair and towing, and restaurants are available in Blanding, Bluff, and Hanksville. Medical care is available at San Juan Hospital in Blanding and in nearby Monticello. Fry Canyon Lodge offers the only gas between Blanding and the gas station/convenience store at Hite Marina on Lake Powell. The lodge also offers a cafe, six guest rooms, ice, propane, and a telephone for emergency use only. Pay telephones are available at Natural Bridges National Monument and at Hite Marina.

Permits

Backcountry permits are required in the following Cedar Mesa canyons: Grand Gulch, Slickhorn Canyons, Fish Canyon, Owl Canyon, North and South Forks of Mule Canyon north of UT 95, Road Canyon, Lime Creek, and their tributaries.

During peak seasons, March 1 through June 15 and September 1 through October 31, a small fee is charged per person per day for day-use permits. Overnight permits also require a fee. Day-use permits may be obtained at each trailhead through a self-pay system. All advanced and walk-in overnight permits must be picked up on the day of your trip at the Kane Gulch Ranger Station between 8 a.m. and noon, seven days a week. Advanced overnight permits may be reserved up to ninety days prior to your trip through the Monticello Field Office at (435) 587-1510.

Commercial groups, groups of eight or more people, or groups using pack or saddle stock must obtain their permits by advance reservation through the Monticello Field Office. Walk-in permits will not be issued to these groups.

During the off-season, June 16 through August 31 and November 1 through February 28, similar small fees are charged for day-use permits, and slightly less for overnight permits. All overnight and day-use permits may be self-issued at each trailhead during the off-season.

Overnight permits for commercial groups or groups using pack or saddle stock must be obtained in advance through the Monticello Field Office at (435) 587-1510.

Additionally, annual day-use passes can be purchased at the Monticello Field Office or the Kane Gulch Ranger Station. This pass is good through the calendar year and will cover all passengers in the vehicle.

For more information on the Cedar Mesa region, including the Dark Canyon Primitive Area, visit the Kane Gulch Ranger Station on UT 261, 3.8 miles south of the junction with UT 95, or contact the BLM Monticello Field office in Monticello at (435) 587-1500 or by mail at PO Box 7, Monticello, UT 84535.

In the event of an emergency, dial 911 or call the San Juan County Sheriff at (435) 587-2237.

1 Mule Canyon

This pleasant, easy day hike follows the course of upper Mule Canyon, one of the most accessible canyons in the Cedar Mesa region. Great bulging cliffs of Cedar Mesa sandstone embrace the canyon, which supports an interesting mixture of pinyon–juniper and montane forest environments.

Distance: 6 miles or more, round-trip
Hiking time: 3.5–4 hours
Difficulty: Easy
Trail surface: Boot-worn trails and wash route
Best season: Apr through early June; Sept through Oct
Canine compatibility: Leashed dogs permitted

Water availability: Seasonal intermittent flows in Mule Canyon; treat before drinking, or bring your own.
Hazards: Flash flood danger
Permits: Required
Maps: USGS Hotel Rock and South Long Point; Trails Illustrated Grand Gulch Plateau

Finding the trailhead: From Blanding, follow UT 191 south 3 miles to the junction of US 191 and UT 95. Turn right (west) onto UT 95 and drive 19.3 miles to the signed turnoff for CR 263 (Arch Canyon). If you are coming from the west, the turnoff is 67 miles east of the Hite Marina turnoff on UT 95, 9 miles east of UT 261, and 0.5 mile east of the signed turnoff to Mule Canyon Indian Ruins.

After turning northeast onto CR 263, pass a parking area on the right (south) side of the road after 200 yards. Then descend a short but rough and rocky downgrade to the bridge spanning Mule Canyon, 0.3 mile from UT 95. A turnout on the right (south) side of CR 263 has room for two or three cars.

The Hike

The trail is sandy but well worn and easy to follow, with few obstacles, making it passable even to novice hikers. You will see several well-preserved Anasazi ruins, most of them grain storage structures. The trail leads directly to some ruins— please respect these fragile, ancient structures.

From the bridge spanning Mule Canyon wash, follow either of two obvious trails that descend abruptly to the floor of the shallow canyon. There the trails join and quickly lead to the trailhead register. Beyond the register, the well-defined trail follows the edge of the Mule Canyon arroyo, soon crossing the usually dry wash to the grassy bench on the opposite side.

The canyon is quite shallow at this point, flanked by low walls of Cedar Mesa sandstone. Pinyon and juniper trees cover the north-facing slopes to your left. On south-facing slopes, the woodland is open and sparse.

After about 0.5 mile, where the wash begins a northwest trend, the canyon grows increasingly confined by bulging walls that rise 150 feet to the rims above. Soon, with slickrock underfoot, you begin to follow the floor of the wash. Multiple trails are frequent in this part of the canyon, but the way is straightforward—you simply follow the wash.

The woodland vegetation in the sheltered confines of the canyon is rich and well developed, more typical of a higher and wetter environment. The northwest trend of the canyon allows considerable shade to be cast by the canyon walls, reducing heat, sunlight, and evaporation.

After hiking for about 1.2 miles, keep your eye out for House on Fire Ruins, one of the most interesting ruins in Mule Canyon. Due to an extraordinary pattern in the sandstone above, the ruin seems to have flames shooting out of the ceiling, a phenomenon that is most dramatic in late morning. After 1.7 miles, the first obvious draw opens up on the right (north). Beyond it, Mule Canyon grows deeper, flanked by red-and-white-banded Cedar Mesa slickrock. Most of the ruins you will see are located above the draw.

Groves of Douglas fir soon begin to appear on the southwest rim, while ponderosa pines grow tall and straight on the opposite rim, lending a sense of scale to the depth of the canyon. The trail ahead continues its crisscrossing course across the wash, hugging the banks closely. This sheltered part of Mule Canyon supports an increasing number of tall conifers, which cast ample shade and add the flavor of a mountain environment to the canyon.

After 2.3 miles, the trail winds among the pines and skirts a deep plunge pool on the right side. At this point, the trail begins to deteriorate. A pair of bays (shallow amphitheaters) opens up on the north wall of the canyon after 3 miles, where tall cottonwoods crowd the banks of the wash. The trail essentially disappears around the point just beyond the Twin Bays; the canyon becomes increasingly confined, and a forest of tall conifers is massed on the canyon floor.

Most hikers will be content to end the hike at the Twin Bays and relax in the shadow of pines and firs, or soak in the sunshine on the slickrock, before backtracking to the trailhead.

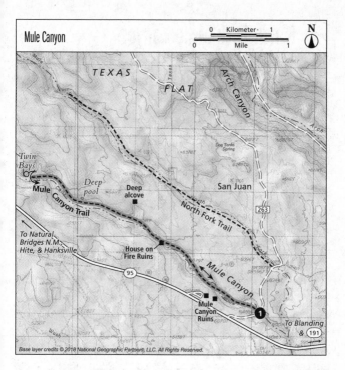

Mule Canyon

Miles and Directions

0.0   Begin hiking at the Mule Canyon trailhead and follow the well-worn path west into the canyon.

1.25 Reach House on Fire Ruins.

2.3   Trail winds through pines and skirts a deep pool.

3.0   Reach the Twin Bays (a set of shallow natural amphitheaters). Return by the same route.

6.0   Arrive back at the trailhead.

2 North Fork Mule Canyon

Much like the main fork of Mule Canyon, the North Fork blends conifer forest and pinyon–juniper woodland with bold slickrock cliffs, providing easy access to a number of fine Anasazi ruins. This fork of the canyon is more confined, and many of its ruins—including dwellings, kivas, and granaries—are better hidden than in the main fork of the canyon, making their discovery more rewarding. Walking in the North Fork is easy and trouble free. Segments of sandy, boot–worn trails guide you upcanyon, and in between you simply follow the wash.

Distance: 5.2 miles or more, round-trip
Hiking time: 2–2.5 hours
Difficulty: Easy
Trail surface: Boot-worn trails and wash route
Best season: Apr through early June; Sept through Oct
Canine compatibility: Leashed dogs permitted

Water availability: Seasonal intermittent flows in the wash; treat before drinking, or bring your own.
Hazards: Flash flood danger
Permits: Required
Maps: USGS Hotel Rock and South Long Point; Trails Illustrated Grand Gulch Plateau

Finding the trailhead: From Blanding, follow US 191 south 3 miles to the junction of US 191 and UT 95. Turn right (west) onto UT 95 and drive 19.3 miles to the signed turnoff for CR 263 (Arch Canyon). If you are coming from the west, the turnoff is 67 miles east of the Hite Marina turnoff on UT 95, 9 miles east of UT 261, and 0.5 mile east of the signed turnoff to Mule Canyon Indian Ruins.

After turning northeast onto CR 263, pass a parking area on the right (south) side of the road after 200 yards. Then descend a short but rough and rocky downgrade to the bridge spanning Mule Canyon, 0.3 mile from UT 95. Continue northwest on CR 263. The road is rough and rocky in places but is easily passable to low-clearance vehicles.

After one switchback, you pass a parking/camping area. At 0.7 mile from UT 95, you pass a corral and undeveloped campsite. The road descends from the corral to the bridge spanning North Fork Mule Canyon, 1 mile from UT 95. Park in the wide spot immediately west of the bridge. Hikers searching for a campsite will find numerous undeveloped sites in the pinyon-juniper woodland along the road, beyond the North Fork.

The Hike

From the southwest abutment of the bridge spanning the North Fork, a well-worn trail gradually descends northwest to the trailhead register. Although the North Fork is more confined than the main fork, the canyon is shallow: only 30 to 40 feet deep for the first 0.5 mile.

The way ahead follows the small wash, where in spring there will likely be flowing water. You will follow segments of trail, but most often you will be walking along the floor of the wash, with slickrock underfoot, occasionally skirting boulders and plunging through willow thickets, forging your own way. Overall, the wash provides a clear avenue to follow upcanyon.

A cooler, sheltered microclimate prevails in the confines of the North Fork, contrasting with the dry woodlands fringing the rims above. Gambel oak, pinyon, and juniper trees stud the slickrock walls above, while on the canyon floor you'll find cottonwoods, ponderosa pines, and Douglas firs.

The bulging, often overhanging red-and-gray-banded Cedar Mesa sandstone cliffs gradually rise higher as you push deeper into the canyon, flanking the North Fork with convoluted 200-foot walls. After 1.9 miles, a prominent wooded draw opens up on the right (north). Just beyond the mouth of the draw is a deep alcove, crowned on its rim by a rust-red sandstone knob. A line of seepage in the alcove supports a ribbon of hanging-garden vegetation, including the brilliant blue flowers of primrose.

The way upcanyon beyond the alcove follows the increasingly confined wash. The forested 8,000-foot plateau of South Long Point, with its distinctive brick-red slopes, rises boldly at the head of the canyon. Look for well-hidden ruins on the ledges and in the alcoves. The trail essentially disappears after 2.6 miles. Most people turn around here and retrace their steps to the trailhead, perhaps finding ruins they missed along the way.

Miles and Directions

0.0 Begin hiking at the North Fork Mule Canyon trailhead and follow the trail northwest to the trailhead register.

1.9 Come to a deep alcove.

2.6 Reach the end of the trail. Turn around and head back to the trailhead.

5.2 Arrive back at the trailhead.

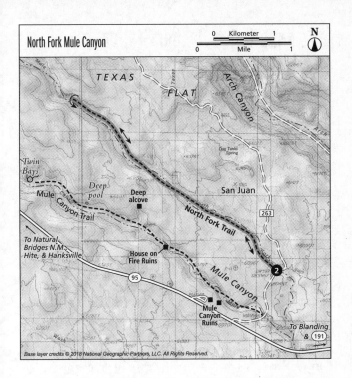

North Fork Mule Canyon

TEXAS FLAT

Arch Canyon

Twin Bays

Deep pool

Deep alcove

Mule Canyon Trail

San Juan

North Fork Trail

263

To Natural Bridges N.M., Hite, & Hanksville

House on Fire Ruins

95

Mule Canyon

Mule Canyon Ruins

2

To Blanding & 191

Base layer credits © 2018 National Geographic Partners, LLC. All Rights Reserved.

3 Kane Gulch Ranger Station to The Junction

Beyond the confines of Utah's national parks, there are hundreds of outstanding canyons that rival those within the parks in their drama and beauty. Among these many canyons, Grand Gulch is one of the finest. Grand Gulch is not only one of the most beautiful canyons in the Glen Canyon region, with its well-developed riparian oases and sculpted sandstone walls, but it also has one of the greatest concentrations of archaeological resources in a single canyon on the Colorado Plateau.

Distance: 8 miles round-trip
Hiking time: 3.5–4.5 hours
Difficulty: Easy to moderate
Trail surface: Constructed and boot-worn trails, generally well defined and easy to follow
Best season: Apr through mid-June; Sept through Oct
Canine compatibility: Leashed dogs permitted
Water availability: Perennial seep below pour-off at 2 miles; seasonal intermittent flows in Grand Gulch; seasonal at Junction Spring, a short distance below Kane Gulch/Grand Gulch confluence; treat before drinking, or bring your own.
Hazards: Flash flood danger
Permits: Required
Maps: USGS Kane Gulch; Trails Illustrated Grand Gulch Plateau

Finding the trailhead: Turn south on UT 261, 56 miles east of the Hite Marina turnoff on UT 95 or 28.3 miles west of the junction of US 191 and UT 95, 3 miles south of Blanding. Drive south on UT 261 for 3.8 miles and park at the trailhead next to the Kane Gulch Ranger Station on the east side of UT 261. If you are driving from the south, the ranger station is 29.2 miles north of the junction of UT 261 and US 163/191 between Mexican Hat and Bluff.

The Hike

Kane Gulch Ranger Station is the jumping-off point for the majority of visitors to Grand Gulch, and the passage of so many hikers' boots keeps the trail well defined and easy to follow. This short trip to the Kane Gulch/Grand Gulch confluence, called "The Junction," not only offers a fine introduction to Grand Gulch, it also affords access to the large cliff dwellings of Junction Ruins and several excellent campsites at the confluence. The trip is suitable as a day hike, an overnighter, or as the first leg of an extended trip into the wild gorge of Grand Gulch.

Backpackers should note that overnight use of The Junction campsites is limited to two consecutive nights. During peak use periods, particularly during Easter week and the month of April, The Junction campsites may be continuously occupied.

From the Kane Gulch Ranger Station parking lot, find the trail on the opposite side of UT 261, indicated by a BLM destination and mileage sign. The trail crosses a sagebrush-studded flat for about 250 yards, then drops to the willow-and clover-fringed banks of Kane Gulch wash. Soon you pass through a gate (leaving it as you find it), cross an expanse of slickrock, then plunge back into the willows, where the trail turns left to follow Kane Gulch downcanyon.

Low walls of white Cedar Mesa sandstone soon border the gradually deepening draw. Scattered cottonwoods and thickets of willow grow vigorously in the bottom of the gulch. Occasional bushwhacking through the willows here is more of a nuisance than it is a challenge.

After about 1 mile, you pass a rare sight in a high desert canyon. Groves of aspen are crowded in the shady recesses beneath the low, north-facing canyon walls, contrasting with the sparse woodland of pinyon and juniper trees that fringes the mesa just above. The nearest montane environment, where aspens typically thrive, is located atop Elk Ridge, 9 miles north and 2,000 feet above Kane Gulch.

After 2 miles, the trail bypasses a major pour-off on the right, then descends steadily over slickrock and a rocky tread back to the canyon floor. A line of seepage emerges from the slickrock beneath the pour-off, sometimes providing enough flow to dampen the wash below.

The trail, compared to canyoneering routes in nearby Cedar Mesa canyons, is pleasant and delightful. The nature of this trail allows you to simply hike and absorb the scenic landscape of this wild canyon.

The gulch attains true canyon proportions below the pour-off, and the rims now rest 300 to 500 feet above the canyon floor. The only vague segment of the trail ensues just below the pour-off, where you follow the wash downcanyon, with slickrock underfoot. Soon you mount another segment of constructed trail that stays high on the north wall of the canyon, following a ledge above a boulder jam and a series of minor pour-offs.

The only steep grade on the hike follows the traverse, where you descend the rocky tread back down to the slickrock wash below. Great alcoves and vaulting cliffs now flank the canyon, and the way ahead through this sandstone corridor alternates between stretches of well-worn trail with a tread of slickrock and sand, and brief trailless segments that follow the wash. There are few obstacles here to impede steady progress.

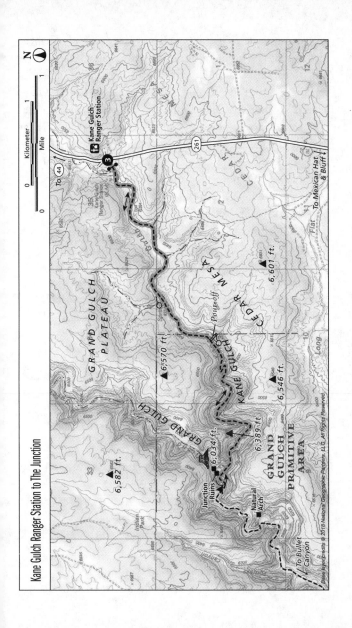

Kane Gulch Ranger Station to The Junction

After 4 miles, Grand Gulch suddenly opens up ahead to the west at The Junction. Its upper reaches, slicing north back into the Grand Gulch Plateau, are quite similar in appearance to Kane Gulch. Straight ahead, Grand Gulch becomes a much wider canyon, flanked by benches studded with cottonwood, pinyon, and juniper trees. An excellent, though popular, camping area lies on a bench at the confluence, while other sites are located just inside Grand Gulch to the north. The campsites, if unoccupied, afford shady resting places for day hikers as well.

Junction Ruins rest in an alcove high on the west wall of Grand Gulch just above The Junction. These well-preserved dwellings consist primarily of slab masonry construction, with one structure displaying wattle-and-daub architecture. To help preserve these ancient structures, hikers should be content to observe them from a distance, perhaps with the aid of binoculars.

After enjoying the peaceful beauty of The Junction, retrace your steps to the trailhead.

Miles and Directions

0.0 Begin hiking southwest on the well-worn trail from the Kane Gulch Ranger Station.

2.0 Reach the pour-off.

4.0 Come to The Junction, the confluence of Kane Gulch and Grand Gulch. Return the way you came.

8.0 Arrive back at the trailhead.

4 Road Canyon

Road Canyon is one of a half-dozen major canyons carved into the eastern flanks of Cedar Mesa draining into Comb Wash. The canyon ranges from 100 to 400 feet deep, embraced by bulging walls of red-and-grey-banded Cedar Mesa sandstone that are sculpted into ledges, alcoves, sheer cliffs, and strange hoodoos. A seasonal stream fringed by a ribbon of riparian foliage, inviting benches shaded by a pygmy forest of pinyon and juniper, the canyon's sculpted slickrock, and the quiet and solitude provided by its remote, off-the-beaten-track location offer ample incentives for visitors to seek out Road Canyon.

Distance: 6.8 miles or more, round-trip
Hiking time: 4 hours or more
Difficulty: Moderately easy
Trail surface: Boot-worn trails and wash route; occasional rudimentary route-finding required
Best season: Apr through mid-June; Sept through Oct
Canine compatibility: Leashed dogs permitted

Water availability: Seasonal intermittent flows in Road Canyon; treat before drinking, or bring your own.
Hazards: Flash flood danger
Permits: Required
Maps: USGS Cedar Mesa North, Snow Flat Spring Cave; Trails Illustrated Grand Gulch Plateau

Finding the trailhead: Turn south on UT 261, 56 miles east of the Hite Marina turnoff on UT 95 or 28.3 miles west of the junction of US 191 and UT 95, 3 miles south of Blanding. Proceed south on UT 261 for 13.5 miles. Turn east onto the road signed for Cigarette Spring, 200 yards north of milepost 19. If you are coming from the south, the turnoff is 23.5 miles north of the junction of UT 261 and US 191/163.

The Cigarette Spring road can be rough in places but should be passable to any vehicle in dry weather. The road leads 1 mile to a gate (leave it open or closed, as you find it), then becomes narrow and winding as it descends to an unsigned junction 3.4 miles from the highway. The right fork leads toward Lime Canyon. Bearing left, continue for about 100 yards, then turn left onto a northbound spur road. Follow the spur 150 yards to the road end and unsigned trailhead, 3.5 miles from UT 261.

Hikers searching for campsites will find a few undeveloped sites near the junction with the road to Lime Canyon and also at the trailhead.

The Hike

Road Canyon not only offers natural beauty but also has many well-preserved Anasazi ruins and rock art. Allow plenty of time for the hike, perhaps an entire day, since you may spend more time here than you expect while scanning hidden recesses for ruins.

The ruins in Road Canyon (and those elsewhere on Cedar Mesa) are threatened by an increase in visitation. Simply walking around ruins can inadvertently cause irreparable damage to the site. Several exceptional kivas in Road Canyon have deteriorated significantly due to human impact since the 1980s. Walk softly when visiting ancient ruins, and treat them with the respect they deserve.

Begin at the road end and follow the trail as it winds a way through the pinyon-juniper woodland, gradually descending across the mesa top. Please stay on the trail here to avoid crushing the well-developed cryptobiotic soil crust. After about 250 yards, the trail begins a gentle descent above a wooded draw carving into the Cedar Mesa sandstone. Here the woodland opens up to reveal the shallow upper reaches of Road Canyon below.

Soon you reach a steep, but brief, descent of 120 feet to the boulder-littered floor of Road Canyon. Look for the cairn indicating this exit trail upon returning. Turn right and head downcanyon, through the wash, over segments of boot-worn trail interspersed with slickrock.

Pinyon and juniper trees cloak the broken sandstone walls in the upper reaches of the canyon, sharing space with their typical companion shrubs: Utah serviceberry, alder leaf mountain mahogany, yucca, Mormon tea, little leaf mountain mahogany, and the silver foliage of roundleaf buffaloberry.

Boulders are massed on the canyon floor at 0.6 mile, and cottonwoods and willow thickets appear as you follow trail segments through this rocky stretch. You must forge your way through the willows at times, but the thickets present more of an inconvenience than a challenge.

After you skirt a deep pothole in the wash, the northwest fork of Road Canyon joins on the left at 0.8 mile. After a few more bends of the canyon, a bold red hoodoo, capped by a gray sandstone slab, projects into the canyon from the north wall. Observant hikers will likely spot several ruins high on the canyon walls along the following 3 miles. As you continue downcanyon, narrow benches studded with pinyons and junipers begin to flank the wash, inviting you to return another time with overnight gear to pass a night or two in the canyon.

Although the walking is generally easy, there are places where you may have to stop and backtrack a few yards to find the best route around an obstacle, typical of canyon hiking in southern Utah. The canyon grows increasingly deeper as you proceed, flanked by 200- to 300-foot cliffs of convoluted sandstone, streaked with desert varnish. Grassy banks often fringe the wash, while a ribbon of cottonwoods, willows, and an occasional tamarisk follow you downcanyon.

After 2.5 miles, the serpentine canyon becomes much more confined, and you are eventually confronted by a typical Cedar Mesa pour-off, with a deep but ephemeral pool below it, at 3.4 miles. Some hikers may elect to backtrack at this point, but if you are determined to continue to more ruins farther downcanyon, bear right and follow a shelf beneath an overhang, following a course that takes you well above the wash.

The route ahead follows the shelf for about 0.5 mile, beyond which a steep slickrock friction pitch and a brief downclimb are necessary to regain the wash. The canyon below is much deeper, with colorful banded sandstone walls reaching 400 to 500 feet to the rims above. After 5.6 miles, just downcanyon from a northwest-trending side canyon, are some of the last ruins in Road Canyon. Most day hikers who have persevered this far will turn around at this point and retrace the route through this scenic canyon to the trailhead.

Miles and Directions

0.0 Begin hiking at the end of the Cigarette Spring road, and head east toward Road Canyon.

0.4 Enter Road Canyon.

3.4 Reach the pour-off. Turn around and retrace your route.

6.8 Arrive back at the trailhead.

Road Canyon

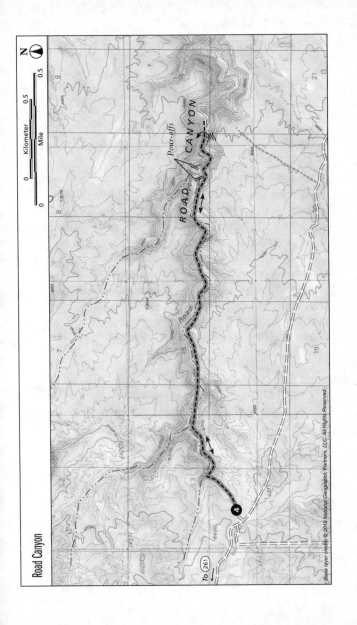

5 Government Trail to Grand Gulch

Government Trail to Grand Gulch offers an excellent hike into the Grand Gulch Primitive Area. Hikers are rewarded with amazing views, a wealth of archaeological sites, and one of the most beautiful desert canyons in the region.

Distance: 6.4 miles round-trip
Hiking time: About 3 hours
Difficulty: Moderately easy
Trail surface: Closed road to the rim of Grand Gulch; constructed trail into the canyon bottom
Best season: Apr through early June; Sept through Oct
Canine compatibility: Leashed dogs permitted
Water availability: Seasonal intermittent flows in Grand Gulch; seasonal Polly's Spring emerges from inside Polly's Canyon, 0.2 mile north (upcanyon) of the foot of the trail; treat before drinking or bring your own.
Hazards: Flash flood danger in Grand Gulch
Permits: Required
Maps: USGS Polly's Pasture; Trails Illustrated Grand Gulch Plateau

Finding the trailhead: From the junction of UT 95 and UT 261, 56 miles east of the Hite Marina turnoff and 28.3 miles west of the UT 95/US 191 junction (3 miles south of Blanding), proceed south on UT 261. Pass the Kane Gulch Ranger Station after 3.8 miles, where updated information on trail and road conditions is available. After 13.5 miles, about 200 yards north of milepost 19, turn right onto a westbound dirt road, opposite the turnoff for the road to Cigarette Spring.

Follow this road west for 0.4 mile where you find a register and an information signboard. The usually good, graded dirt road ahead has a few rough and rocky stretches, and barring severe runoff damage, it remains passable to passenger cars in dry weather. After 2.6 miles you reach a prominent but unsigned junction, where you turn right (west). The good, graded road leads west across the mesa, offering splendid views of the Red House Cliffs, Tables of the Sun, Navajo Mountain, and the distant Kaiparowits Plateau.

You reach a signed junction after 3 miles (5.6 miles from UT 261), where you bear right onto graded CR 245. Follow this road for 1.9 miles, then turn right (west) onto a narrow spur road signed for Government Trail. This poor road has high centers in places but remains passable to cars for about 0.5 mile. If you have a low-clearance, 2WD car, park in one of the wide spots on the slickrock at that point and walk the remaining distance to the trailhead. If you are in a high-clearance, 4WD vehicle, continue down the very rough and rocky road for the final 0.6 mile to the signed trailhead, 1.2 miles from CR 245, next to a willow-fringed stock pond. Hikers searching for a campsite have innumerable undeveloped sites to choose from en route to the trailhead.

The Hike

Constructed by the BLM in the 1970s, the Government Trail is the second shortest and has the easiest access into Grand Gulch. The route follows a long-closed road over the shrub-dotted expanse of Polly's Pasture, near the southwestern edge of the Cedar Mesa/Polly Mesa tableland, then descends 300 feet via a well-constructed trail into the middle reaches of Grand Gulch. The hike is a rewarding day trip but is most frequently used by backpackers as part of an extended trip in Grand Gulch. At the end of the road, adjacent to the stock pond, is an information signboard displaying maps, backcountry regulations, and abundant tips on Leave No Trace.

Ample signs indicate the trail, which begins by crossing the dam of the willow-fringed pond. Just beyond, you curve left and skirt the bed of an abandoned Studebaker pickup. The first 2.7 miles of the way follow the doubletrack of a long-closed road, and signs at the trailhead ask hikers to walk in the left track only; unfortunately, few hikers do. As long as hikers keep walking in both tracks, the old road will remain a lasting, well-defined scar on the mesa.

Vistas from the open mesa are far-ranging and panoramic. The brick-red Bears Ears and Woodenshoe Buttes rise on the far northern horizon, defining the southern rim of lofty Elk Ridge. Moss Back Butte and the Tables of the Sun anchor the northern end of the Red House Cliffs to the northwest. The cliffs of Red Canyon, a prominent gap in the Red House Cliffs, frame a fine view of distant Mounts Holmes, Hillers, and Pennell in the Henry Mountains. And to the southwest, the sweeping ocher faces of the Red House Cliffs point to the dome of Navajo Mountain, over 50 miles distant.

The gently contoured platform of Polly's Pasture is covered in a veneer of red soil, with only widely scattered outcrops of Cedar Mesa sandstone punctuating the mesa. A few pinyons and junipers dot the mesa, which is dominated by a ground-cover of blackbrush.

Punctuating the mesa top in the distance are broad exposures of white Cedar Mesa sandstone, yet there is little indication of a canyon lying across your path. Except for the slickrock ahead, the mesa seemingly stretches uninterrupted to the foot of the Red House Cliffs.

Midway to the rim of Grand Gulch, the road briefly disappears as you mount slickrock, where cairns point the way to the resumption of the doubletrack ahead. Soon, overhanging cliffs come into view at the rim of Grand Gulch in the southwest and Polly's Canyon to the north. After 2.7 miles of road walking, you reach the slickrock rim of Grand Gulch at 5,370 feet, where a large BLM sign proclaims "Government Trail, Grand Gulch Primitive Area."

Grand Gulch opens up before you, a 300-foot-deep gorge embraced by sweeping walls of cross-bedded Cedar Mesa slickrock. Across the narrow gulf of the gulch rises the erosion-isolated butte of Polly's Island, cut off from the opposite rim by an abandoned meander of the Grand Gulch stream course.

The well-defined constructed trail descends a moderate grade below the rim via switchbacks. In some places the trail is rocky, and in others the trail has been carved into the bulging slickrock. Six switchbacks lead down to the brow

of a pour-off, where the trail turns left (southwest) and begins a lengthy traverse. Soon, a series of short switchbacks lead steeply down to the floor of Grand Gulch. Once you reach the gulch, you can roam at will. There is a wealth of archaeological sites here, but, the Anasazi sites notwithstanding, Grand Gulch is arguably one of the most beautiful desert canyons in the region.

After enjoying your visit to Grand Gulch, retrace your route to the trailhead.

Miles and Directions

0.0 Follow the signs pointing out the trail and hike northwest across Polly's Pasture.

2.7 Reach the rim of Grand Gulch.

3.2 Reach the floor of Grand Gulch. Return by the same route.

6.4 Arrive back at the trailhead.

6 Sipapu Bridge to Kachina Bridge

The natural bridges of White Canyon were known by the Navajo and Paiute long before European settlers came to Utah. The Anasazi lived among the bridges in White Canyon, and hikers today visit the canyon not only to explore the unique natural spans of stone but also to see Anasazi ruins and rock art. This memorable half-day hike surveys the two largest natural bridges in the monument, separated by the dramatic, bulging Cedar Mesa sandstone cliffs of White Canyon. En route, the trail passes Horse Collar Ruin, an example of an unusual style of Anasazi architecture. The trail loops back to the trailhead via the mesa top, thus surveying the entire spectrum of monument landscapes.

Distance: 5-mile loop
Hiking time: 3-4 hours
Difficulty: Moderately easy
Trail surface: Constructed trail, well defined and easy to follow
Best season: Apr through mid-June; Sept through Oct
Canine compatibility: Dogs not permitted

Water availability: Bring your own.
Hazards: Flash flood danger
Permits: Not required
Maps: *USGS Moss Back Butte; Trails Illustrated Dark Canyon/ Manti-La Sal National Forest*

Finding the trailhead: Follow UT 95 for 30.1 miles west from the US 191/UT 95 junction (3 miles south of Blanding), or 42.5 miles east from the Hite Marina turnoff on UT 95, to northbound UT 275, prominently signed for Natural Bridges National Monument and Manti-La Sal National Forest-Elk Ridge Access.

This paved, two-lane road leads first north, then generally west, passing the turnoff to Elk Ridge after 0.6 mile and Deer Flat Road after 1 mile. You enter Natural Bridges National Monument at 3.8 miles and reach the visitor center 4.5 miles from UT 95. Pay the entrance fee inside the visitor center before proceeding.

Beyond the visitor center you pass the campground and reach the 8.5-mile, one-way loop road Bridge View Drive (open 7 a.m. to 9 p.m. daily) after 0.5 mile and bear right. The signed Sipapu trailhead parking area is located 2 miles from the beginning of the loop road.

The Hike

A visit to Natural Bridges National Monument is a must for anyone traveling on UT 95 across Cedar Mesa. Located near the head of White Canyon, a 40-mile tributary to the Colorado River carving through the resistant Cedar Mesa sandstone, the bridges in the monument are among the largest in the world.

Cass Hite, historical prospector and operator of the Hite Crossing ferry on the Colorado River, claimed to have seen the natural stone bridges of White Canyon in 1883. J. A. Scorup, who ranged cattle across one of the largest ranches in Utah, visited the bridges in 1895. A later trip to the bridges guided by Scorup resulted in magazine articles that focused the nation's interest on preserving the unique landscape. In 1908, President Theodore Roosevelt created Natural Bridges National Monument, the first national monument to be established in Utah.

From the Sipapu trailhead, the trail begins as a rock-outlined slickrock route, descending over the White Canyon rim. The way quickly evolves into a constructed trail, carved into the slickrock, with steps in places that afford better footing. Once below the rim, the trail traverses beneath an overhang to the top of a steel stairway that affords passage over an otherwise impassable cliff band. Tall Douglas firs, a montane tree common on southern Utah plateaus above 8,000 feet, thrive in the cool microclimates of shady niches on the north-facing canyon walls below.

Soon you reach a second stairway that offers an exciting passage over a 20-foot cliff. Just below the stairway, descend a tall, sturdy wooden ladder, then follow the trail as it curves out to a fine viewpoint on a sandstone ledge at 6,000 feet, overlooking Sipapu Bridge. The trail then descends steadily, via switchbacks among Cedar Mesa slabs, upon slopes studded with pinyon pines, junipers, Gambel oaks, and the spreading shrubs of Utah serviceberry.

You regain the slickrock below at the south abutment of Sipapu Bridge, which now towers above you. Descend two short but steep slickrock friction pitches, with the aid of handrails and two short ladders, then reach level ground beneath the bridge in White Canyon wash, about thirty minutes and 0.5 mile from the trailhead. A trail register is located in a Gambel oak grove beneath the bridge, alongside the cottonwood-fringed banks of the wash.

The bridge was formed as the waters of White Canyon abandoned a meander in the streambed and carved a more direct course through a thin wall of sandstone. This mature bridge, the largest in the monument, is no longer being enlarged by stream erosion, since its abutments now rest high above the wash. In its dimensions, Sipapu is second only to Rainbow Bridge in Glen Canyon and thus bears the distinction of being the second largest natural bridge in the world. The bridge's dimensions are listed on the trail register.

To continue, cross the seasonal stream beneath the towering span of Sipapu and follow the well-worn trail downcanyon, crossing the wash three more times en route to Deer Canyon. The trail ahead is a delightful walk through spectacular White Canyon. The bulging, mostly white walls of Cedar Mesa sandstone present an ever-changing scene of sheer cliffs, alcoves, ledges, and towers sculpted into fanciful forms by ages of weathering and erosion.

Deer Canyon opens up on the right (north) 1 mile from the trailhead. Don't miss the short side trip to Horse Collar Ruin about five minutes and 250 yards below the mouth of Deer Canyon. A steep slickrock scramble is necessary to reach the deep alcove that houses an unusual collection of small Anasazi dwellings and granaries.

Resuming your trek downcanyon on the well-defined trail, you will cross the wash five more times en route to Kachina Bridge. When you spy a small angular arch adjacent to blocky Ruin Rock on the southern skyline, only a few more bends of the canyon separate you from Kachina Bridge.

When you reach the bridge, notice the wooded draw branching left (northeast). That draw is an abandoned mean-der, the ancestral course of White Canyon, now resting several feet above today's stream course. Much like the formation of Sipapu Bridge, the stream abandoned its former course and carved a more direct route, creating the opening of Kachina Bridge in the thin wall of sandstone. Kachina is the youngest of the monument's bridges, and stream erosion is still at work enlarging the span.

There are multiple trails at Kachina Bridge, so to stay on course you should cross the wash twice beneath the bridge and head toward the trail register at the eastern abutment, where you will find a fine petroglyph panel.

After carving through Kachina Bridge, White Canyon begins a northwestward course toward its eventual confluence with Lake Powell. The trail, however, continues southbound, now ascending the White Canyon tributary of Armstrong Canyon. About 250 yards beyond Kachina Bridge, the trail to the rim, indicated by a small sign, begins ascending slickrock to the left, with the aid of carved steps and handrails. Avoid the path that continues up Armstrong Canyon on the right side of the wash, since it soon dead-ends at a pour-off.

After the brief slickrock ascent ends, you traverse a short distance to a signed junction. The trail to the right continues ascending Armstrong Canyon, eventually leading to Owachomo Bridge. You should bear left, however, toward the Kachina parking area, gaining 300 feet in the following 0.5 mile, the steepest part of the hike. This trail ascends steeply at times, via rock steps and a series of short, tight switchbacks. Views expand with every step, revealing the red, layered Organ Rock shale that caps the wooded mesas above. Although Kachina Bridge remains in view for much of the ascent, its angle of repose and shadows often give it the appearance of a large alcove rather than a great span of stone.

At length the trail levels off as you curve around a bulging, mushroom-shaped knob just below the rim and mount slickrock, ascending several yards to the paved Kachina Overlook Trail. Bear right to reach the parking area and loop road after 100 yards, at 6,032 feet.

The trail resumes on the opposite (east) side of the road, winding over the corrugated mesa top with a gradual uphill trend. Pinyons and junipers form a widely scattered woodland here because of the competition for scant available moisture. Understory shrubs are widely separated, in sharp contrast to the rich vegetation in the canyon below.

Views from the mesa reach far down White Canyon to Mount Ellen in the Henry Mountains, to Deer Flat and the brick-red Woodenshoe Buttes in the northwest and north, and southwest to the square-edged platform of Moss Back Butte.

After 0.9 mile, turn left (north) at the signed junction, heading toward Sipapu trailhead. Much of White Canyon disappears from view as you proceed north through the woodland. Be sure to stick to the trail while hiking across the mesa; otherwise, the well-developed cryptobiotic soil crust will bear the marks of your passing for a generation.

Soon the northbound trail descends 120 feet into a prominent draw incised into the mesa. Enjoy the view of the twin buttes of the Bears Ears before dropping into the draw. Beyond the draw you briefly follow a steadily ascending

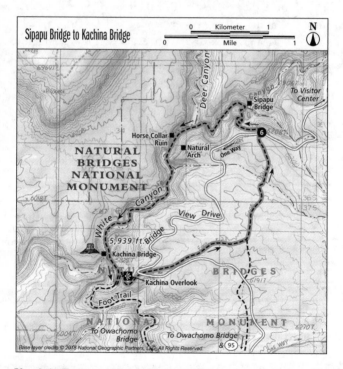

cairned route over a broad expanse of slickrock, then resume your hike on good trail leading through the woodland.

At length, White Canyon opens up below you to the north, and you descend the final few yards to the Sipapu trailhead.

Miles and Directions

0.0 From the Sipapu trailhead, head north toward Sipapu Bridge.

0.5 Come to Sipapu Bridge.

1.2 Arrive at Horse Collar Ruin.

2.6 Come to Kachina Bridge.

2.9 Reach Kachina Bridge Trail and turn left.

3.3 Come to the Kachina Bridge trailhead and cross the road to find the mesa trail.

4.2 Arrive at the junction with southbound trail leading to Owachomo Bridge Trailhead and bear left (north).

5.0 Arrive back at the trailhead.

7 Collins Spring Trailhead to The Narrows

Grand Gulch, a rich riparian oasis and outdoor museum of the ancient Anasazi culture, is one of Utah's classic canyons, yet its remote setting is largely reserved for the backpacker willing to spend several days exploring its hidden depths. A notable exception is the easy walk down Collins Canyon to The Narrows, perhaps the best short hike in Grand Gulch. This fine trip traces the slickrock gorge of Collins Canyon, the only Grand Gulch access from the west, via a well-worn, and in places constructed, trail into the lower reaches of Grand Gulch.

Distance: 4 miles round-trip

Hiking time: 2.5–3 hours

Difficulty: Easy

Trail surface: Constructed and boot-worn trails, well defined

Best season: Apr through early June; Sept through Oct

Canine compatibility: Dogs not permitted

Water availability: Seasonal intermittent flows in Grand Gulch; bring your own.

Hazards: Flash flood danger

Permits: Required

Maps: *USGS Red House Spring; Trails Illustrated Grand Gulch Plateau; BLM Grand Gulch Primitive Area*

Finding the trailhead: Follow UT 95 to the junction with southbound UT 276, signed for Lake Powell, Halls Crossing, and Bullfrog via ferry. This junction is located between mileposts 83 and 84 on UT 95 and is 83.8 miles southeast of Hanksville, 34.9 miles east of the turnoff to Hite Marina, and 37.7 miles west of the US 191/UT 95 junction (3 miles south of Blanding).

Follow UT 276 south across the rolling, wooded mesa beneath the Red House Cliffs. After leaving the woodland, the highway emerges onto a shrub-dotted terrace. You will pass milepost 85, 6.4 miles south of UT 95. There, begin looking for a large, solitary juniper tree on the right (west) side of the highway. About 200 yards beyond the juniper and 0.3 mile beyond milepost 85, turn left (east) onto an unsigned dirt road. A BLM sign a short distance down this road points to Collins Canyon, and another sign designates the route as CR 260 (Gulch Creek).

This good, graded dirt road affords memorable views of Navajo Mountain, Monument Valley, and the slickrock labyrinth of Grand Gulch. After 2.4 miles, bear right at an unsigned junction. Slickrock appears in the roadbed after 4.4 miles, making for a bumpy ride and dictating careful driving for hikers approaching in a low-clearance vehicle.

The road ends at the signed trailhead 6.5 miles from UT 276. Hikers arriving late in the day will find two excellent undeveloped campsites en route to the trailhead, or one may camp at the trailhead. In Grand Gulch, dogs are not allowed downstream from the confluence with Collins Canyon.

The Hike

From the trailhead on the rim of the mesa above Collins Canyon, exciting views can be had into the slickrock-embraced gorge, luring you onto the trail that begins behind the information signboard and trailhead register. At once the trail descends moderately via three short switchbacks over the first band of Cedar Mesa sandstone and into the infant canyon below. There you gently descend over the corrugated slopes above the draw of Collins Canyon.

Soon you pass the mouth of a shallow northeast-trending draw and travel through a wooden gate that bars cattle from entering Collins Canyon and Grand Gulch. Be sure to keep the gate closed. A brief, moderately descending segment of constructed trail, the steepest grade on the hike, ensues beyond the gate. The trail drops down a dugway, a trail carved into a cliff or steep slope, into the wash below.

Upon reaching the wash, the tread becomes obscure. Simply follow the wash ahead for about 150 yards to the lip of a major pour-off. Cairns should be in place to direct you around the pour-off to the right (south) and onto another dugway, where the trail has been carved into the canyon wall. Another short, moderately steep grade leads you back to the canyon floor. Here you'll notice that the drainage has evolved from a draw just above the pour-off into a true canyon, now 200 feet deep.

Collins Canyon is embraced by tall, bulging, red-and-tan-banded walls of Cedar Mesa slickrock. Domes, towers, balanced rocks, and sculpted hoodoos cap the overhanging canyon rims. Pinyon pines, junipers, and Gambel oaks are scattered across the canyon floor, and the occasional cottonwood fringes the wash. Nearly every bend in the canyon presents a shady over-hang, inviting a cool respite from the sun on the hike out.

After four bends of the canyon below the pour-off, the trail edges close to a small but distinctive arch. Be sure to take note of a north-trending side canyon that opens up on the left after 1.5 miles. On your way back to the trailhead, bear left at that confluence, making sure that you don't turn into that canyon, which is similar in depth and appearance to Collins Canyon.

After rounding the next bend ahead, Grand Gulch opens up below and soon you reach a shrub-studded bench at the mouth of Collins Canyon at 4,760 feet, 1.8 miles from the trailhead. There are two ways to reach The Narrows from this point. One route follows the rocky, sandy, and perhaps muddy wash of Grand Gulch downcanyon to the right (south) for 0.2 mile. An easier way follows a boot-worn,

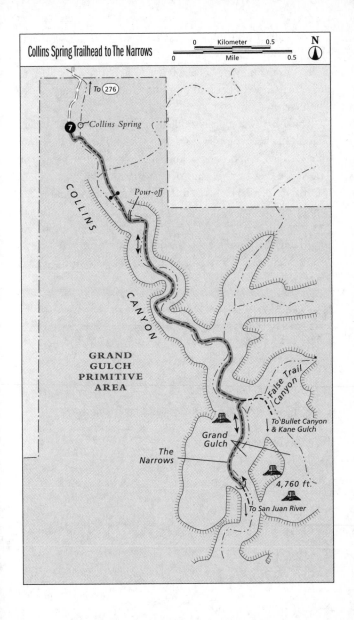

Collins Spring Trailhead to The Narrows

Kilometer 0 — 0.5
Mile 0 — 0.5

N

To (276)

○ Collins Spring

7

COLLINS

Pour-off

CANYON

GRAND
GULCH
PRIMITIVE
AREA

False Trail
Canyon

To Bullet Canyon
& Kane Gulch

Grand
Gulch

The
Narrows

4,760 ft.

To San Juan River

occasionally brushy trail across the bench on the west side of the Grand Gulch wash. Find that trail from the mouth of Collins Canyon by heading south across the canyon's wash to the bench above. That trail dips into Grand Gulch just above The Narrows.

The Narrows appear suddenly and unexpectedly, where Grand Gulch's stream has carved a passage through a narrow, finlike ridge, abandoning a long meander in the streambed. The shade cast by the walls of The Narrows and its shallow, seasonal pool make this a fine, peaceful destination on the sandy banks of the wash beneath the fluttering foliage of small cottonwoods. Great bulging cliffs soar 300 feet overhead, amplifying the music of the small seasonal stream.

After enjoying this tranquil locale, retrace your steps to the trailhead.

Miles and Directions

0.0 Begin hiking southeast at the Collins Spring Trailhead into Collins Canyon.

1.8 Come to the confluence of Collins Canyon and Grand Gulch; turn right, hiking downcanyon.

2.0 Reach The Narrows. Turn around and return the way you came.

4.0 Arrive back at the trailhead.

8 North Wash to Marinus Canyon

Marinus Canyon is a classic, dry desert gorge, embraced by fluted 600-foot walls of Wingate sandstone. The low elevations of the canyon make it a fine choice for an early spring or late autumn outing, when higher canyons, such as those on Cedar Mesa, are too snowy or cold. There are no trails here; you simply follow the dry wash upcanyon. Although the route is generally easy to follow, the wash is sandy and for much of the way you'll be rock-hopping and weaving among boulders. At the end of the canyon's right fork is a shady overhang supporting hanging gardens, offering a fine destination for a half-day hike.

Distance: 7 miles round-trip
Hiking time: About 4 hours
Difficulty: Moderately easy
Trail surface: Wash route
Best season: Mid-Mar through mid-May; mid-Sept through mid-Nov

Canine compatibility: Dogs permitted
Water availability: Bring your own.
Hazards: Flash flood danger
Permits: Not required
Maps: *USGS Hite North*

Finding the trailhead: Drive southeast 34.6 miles from Hanksville on UT 95 or northwest 12.3 miles from the Hite Marina turnoff on UT 95, 1.7 miles north of the Glen Canyon National Recreation Area boundary. This unsigned, easy-to-miss canyon opens up on the east side of UT 95 in North Wash canyon, 0.4 mile north of milepost 35 and 0.6 mile south of milepost 34.

Avoid the very narrow track that leads about 100 feet across a small earthen dam at the mouth of Marinus Canyon. Instead, park off the highway in one of the wide spots near the canyon mouth.

The Hike

Enter the mouth of Marinus Canyon via the small earthen dam, then simply make your way up the rocky, boulder-strewn wash. A scattering of Fremont cottonwoods, tamarisks, and rabbitbrush fringe the usually dry wash, while the green foliage of single-leaf ash and apache plume, with its white spring blossoms and feathery summer fruits, dot the slopes above.

The wash begins amid the rocks of the Chinle Formation. Shortly after entering the canyon mouth, you must briefly scramble up to the left of a resistant green ledge cutting across the wash, the only significant obstacle in the canyon.

Tall, fluted cliffs of Wingate sandstone, often coated with a metallic blue veneer of desert varnish, embrace the confined canyon, with the reddish-brown ledges and cliff bands of Kayenta Formation rocks capping the rims. The lower slopes of the canyon are composed of the varicolored Chinle Formation rocks, the colorful beds hidden behind a mask of coarse desert shrubs and great sandstone blocks fallen from the cliffs above.

After gradually ascending this quiet, majestic canyon for 2 miles, you can see the confluence of two branches of the canyon a short distance ahead. Just before reaching the confluence, the wash is choked with huge boulders for about 100 yards. It is not too difficult to pick a way through this obstacle, with only minor scrambling necessary.

When you reach the forks of the canyon after another 0.2 mile, at 4,275 feet, follow the right fork. In the left fork, a boulder jam makes further travel difficult at best. The right fork ahead offers clear sailing, save for an occasional minor boulder jam and rock-strewn stretches.

As you proceed, the Wingate sandstone walls steadily close in and further confine the gorge. After passing above the

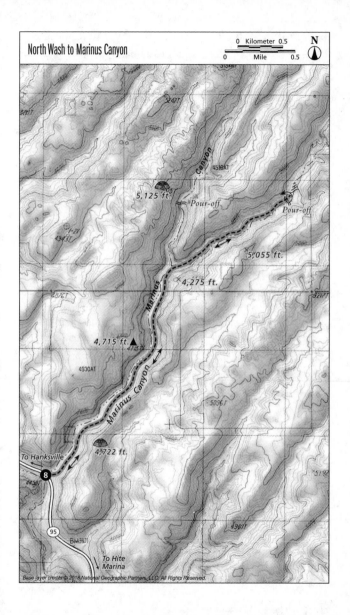

North Wash to Marinus Canyon

0 Kilometer 0.5

0   Mile   0.5

N

5,125 ft.
Pour-off
Pour-off
5,055 ft.
4,275 ft.
4,715 ft. ▲
4930AT
Marinus Canyon
4,722 ft.
To Hanksville
8
95
BM 3521
To Hite
Marina

topmost layer of the Chinle Formation, the Wingate reaches down to the canyon floor, and the drainage grows increasingly narrow as it slices back into this resistant sandstone.

After hiking about one hour and 1.25 miles from the forks of the canyon, you reach a low pour-off blocking further progress. Beneath the pour-off is a shady overhang, supporting a seep line decorated with the delicate fronds of maidenhair fern. During wet seasons, you will find a deep pool below the pour-off.

The canyon slots up ahead, and determined hikers can bypass the pour-off on the left and continue upcanyon. Most hikers, however, will likely be content to turn around at the pour-off and retrace their steps through Marinus Canyon to the trailhead.

Miles and Directions

0.0 Follow the narrow track that leads about 100 feet across a small earthen dam at the mouth of Marinus Canyon.

2.2 Reach forks of Marinus Canyon and follow the right fork.

3.5 Reach pour-off and alcove. Return by the same route.

7.0 Arrive back at the trailhead.

$\textcircled{9}$ Hog Springs Rest Area to Hog Canyon

Hog Springs Rest Area offers a pleasant stopover featuring two picnic sites with awnings and tables and a restroom nearby. The short stroll up Hog Canyon from the rest area offers a more intimate association with a dramatic desert canyon than the scenic UT 95 can provide. One mile up the canyon, far beyond the noise of highway traffic, a deep pool and a small waterfall in the shade of a deep alcove offer an attractive destination for a short hike on a warm spring or autumn day.

Distance: 2 miles round-trip
Hiking time: About 1.5 hours
Difficulty: Easy
Trail surface: Boot-worn trails and wash route
Best season: Mid-Mar through mid-May; mid-Sept through mid-Nov

Canine compatibility: Dogs permitted
Water availability: Bring your own.
Hazards: Flash flood danger
Permits: Not required
Maps: *USGS Hite North, Black Table*

Finding the trailhead: The trailhead is located at the prominently signed Hog Springs Rest Area alongside UT 95 between mileposts 33 and 34, 14.6 miles northwest of the turnoff to Hite Marina and 33.3 miles southeast of Hanksville.

The Hike

From the large rest area parking lot, cross the bridge spanning North Wash and enter the picnic site. Immediately before reaching the second picnic table, follow the trail that descends to the banks of the small stream. Cross the stream and proceed upcanyon via the slopes above the wash on the right. Bold slickrock walls of orange Wingate sandstone, dimpled with solution cavities, bound the lower reaches of the narrow canyon.

The trail begins as an obvious boot-worn path, but recent flash flood activity will determine how well defined you find it. If the way is faint or occasionally nonexistent, simply follow above the banks of the wash, shortcutting its meanders via streamside benches. Avoid the rich growth of grasses and rushes, where seepage creates a mire along the wash banks.

Great rounded cliffs of Navajo Sandstone soon appear at the head of the canyon on the rim of Trachyte Point. The sheer Wingate walls diminish in height as you work your way up the canyon, and the cliffs of Kayenta rocks replace the Wingate with their rubble ledges mantled with coarse desert shrubs and low cliff bands. Navajo domes crown the canyon rims.

After 1 mile, listen for the music of running water. Pick your way through a short rock-strewn stretch of the wash to the source of that sound, hidden until the end behind a screen of tall willows. Then, suddenly, you will reach the wide pool lying beneath the overhang of a shady alcove. A 6-foot waterfall, draining the perennial springs issuing from the upper canyon, plunges into the pool over a resistant ledge of Kayenta sandstone. Mosses and fronds of maidenhair fern decorate the moist walls of the alcove, where seeping water drips like rain into the pool and onto the sandy beach beside it.

After enjoying this cool, peaceful locale, retrace your route to the trailhead.

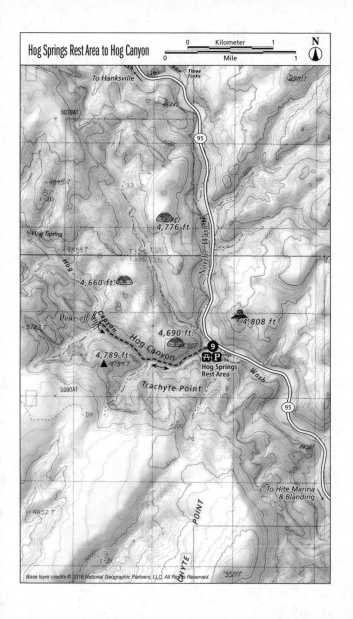

Hog Springs Rest Area to Hog Canyon

To Hanksville

Three Forks

95

North Wash

4,776 ft.

Hog Spring

4,660 ft.

Pour-off

Hog Canyon

4,690 ft.

4,789 ft.

9

Hog Springs Rest Area

Wash

Trachyte Point

95

To Hite Marina & Blanding

TRACHYTE POINT

Miles and Directions

0.0 Follow the trail from the picnic site, crossing a small stream and proceeding upcanyon (above the wash on the right).

1.0 Reach the pool and pour-off. Turn around and retrace your steps.

2.0 Arrive back at the trailhead.

The Escalante Canyons

The Escalante canyons are the premier hiking destination in the Glen Canyon region, and the reason can probably be summed up in one word: slickrock. From broad washes in the Circle Cliffs basin and on the Straight Cliffs/Hole-in-the-Rock terrace and mountain streams high on the flanks of Boulder Mountain, the canyons of the Escalante River drainage quickly develop into a network of slickrock gorges that are the veins feeding the artery of the river. Although the Escalante River courses some 80 miles through a wilderness canyon of incomparable beauty, travel down its gorge is often brutal, a test of endurance for even the most experienced canyoneer. Its tributary canyons are equally attractive and are the primary destinations of most hikers visiting the region.

Navajo Sandstone is the predominant rock formation in the Escalante canyons, and erosion has exhumed these ancient sand dunes and sculpted the resistant cross-bedded slickrock into a vast landscape of domes incised with innumerable serpentine canyons. Nowhere else in the canyon country of the Colorado Plateau is there such an immense expanse of slickrock. The unique landscape, reliable water in many canyons, and hiking routes that traverse the spectrum of difficulty combine to make the Escalante region an increasingly popular alternative destination to the national parks of Utah.

The unique beauty of the Escalante region was recognized as early as 1866, yet the area somehow escaped achieving national-park status in the ensuing years. After the floodgates closed on Glen Canyon Dam in 1963, the lower Escalante canyons were lost beneath the waters of Lake Powell. In 1972 these canyons were included within the boundaries of Glen Canyon National Recreation Area, managed under the direction of the National Park Service. With the establishment of the 1.7-million-acre Grand Staircase–Escalante National Monument in 1996 and the limited protection that designation provides, all of the Escalante canyons are at last held in trust for the benefit and enjoyment of future generations.

Typical of the canyon country of southern Utah, there are few established trails in the Escalante canyons. Most hikes follow the corridors of washes or cross open expanses of slickrock. The exception is the trail to Lower Calf Creek Falls, one of the few constructed and maintained trails in the Glen Canyon region.

There aren't many easy hikes in the Escalante region, yet the few that qualify as best easy day hikes are outstanding. Active waterfalls, arches, narrow canyons, riparian oases, and sculpted slickrock are among the attractions of the Escalante's easy day hikes.

Camping

The two public campgrounds in Grand Staircase–Escalante National Monument are located in the Escalante region. The seven-unit Deer Creek Campground, located on Burr Trail Road 6.2 miles southeast of UT 12 and Boulder, is open year-round and is available for a fee on a first-come, first-served basis. Set among willows and cottonwoods in the canyon of perennial Deer Creek, the site includes tables, fire grills, and pit toilets, but no drinking water.

The fourteen-unit Calf Creek Campground is located just off UT 12 at the Lower Calf Creek Falls trailhead (see Hike 11).

This campground is open year-round for a fee and features the same facilities as the Deer Creek site, though drinking water is available from spring through autumn.

Elsewhere in the monument or national recreation area, you may camp at large, wherever you wish, unless otherwise posted. Roads en route to most trailheads offer spur roads or pullouts where you can park and set up a tent. Always use established sites, and never drive off-road and create new sites. Campfires should be avoided in the monument and are not permitted in Glen Canyon National Recreation Area. See the "Leave No Trace" section in this guide's introduction for more tips on preserving this area.

Access and Services

The only highway providing access to the region is UT 12. This road offers an exceptional scenic drive for 118 miles between UT 24 at Torrey and US 89 south of Panguitch, Utah.

The historic Hole-in-the-Rock Road, branching southeast from UT 12, just east of Escalante, affords access to the west side of the lower Escalante canyons. This is an often rough, remote desert road that is surprisingly busy with both hikers driving to and from trailheads and scenic drivers.

Travel down this road is slow, so expect a drive of several hours en route to some trailheads. The road is subject to washouts and can become impassable during and shortly after heavy rains. I have seen cars stranded on this road for several days following one afternoon of heavy rain. A 4WD vehicle is usually not required but is recommended to safely navigate the road during changing weather conditions, though visitors drive the road in vehicles ranging from compact cars to motor homes.

Obtain up-to-date road information from the Escalante Interagency Visitor Center before driving on Hole-in-the-Rock Road, and be sure you top off your gas tank and have several gallons of water, extra food, and other supplies in the event you become temporarily stranded.

Services in the region are limited to the small towns of Boulder and Escalante. Escalante offers gas, groceries, several motels, restaurants, hiking and camping supplies, auto repair and towing, and a medical clinic. In Boulder there are two gas/convenience stores, restaurants, motels, auto repair, limited groceries, and the Anasazi State Park and Museum. For updated information on road and hiking route conditions, contact the Escalante Interagency Visitor Center at (435) 826-5499, or visit the office at the west end of Escalante on UT 12. The visitor center is open seven days a week, 7:30 a.m. to 5:30 p.m., from mid-March to mid-November. Winter hours are in effect between mid-November and mid-March, 8 a.m. to 4:30 p.m., Monday through Friday.

If an emergency arises, dial 911 or call the Garfield County Sheriff at (435) 676-2678.

10 Upper Calf Creek Falls

Few hikes in the Escalante region offer the rewards of this fine, short trip with such a minimal investment of time and effort. Vast expanses of Navajo Sandstone slickrock and far-ranging vistas, plus an 87-foot-high waterfall, pools of cool water, and shady riparian oases, await hikers following this well-worn trail.

Distance: 2 miles round-trip

Hiking time: 1–1.5 hours

Difficulty: Moderate; Class 2 friction pitches just below the rim

Trail surface: Cairned slickrock route and boot-worn trails

Best season: Apr through early June; Sept through Oct

Canine compatibility: Leashed dogs permitted, but not recommended due to steep terrain near the falls

Water availability: Calf Creek; treat before drinking, or bring your own.

Hazards: Flash flood danger in Calf Creek canyon

Permits: Not required for day hikes

Maps: *USGS Calf Creek; Trails Illustrated Canyons of the Escalante*

Finding the trailhead: This unmarked spur road is located approximately 20.5 miles north of Escalante on UT 12. The dirt road to the trailhead can be found on the north (left) side of the road between mile markers 80 and 81. The very rough and rocky road leads 0.1 mile to the trailhead parking area on the rim of Calf Creek canyon. There are pullouts in which to park just off the highway if you are driving a low-clearance vehicle.

The Hike

Signs at the trailhead proclaim that no camping is permitted there, and that no camping or fires are allowed within 0.5 mile of the upper falls. The trail begins behind these signs and the trailhead register, leading immediately over the rim and to the top of a steep Navajo slickrock slope, littered with round gray volcanic rocks and boulders. The slopes of all the upper Escalante canyons are strewn with these Tertiary rocks, carried in glacial meltwater from their source high on the slopes of Boulder Mountain more than 10,000 years ago.

A swath has been cleared through the rocky veneer, and cairns show the way down the swath via a moderately steep slickrock friction pitch. The route is easier than it first appears, and hikers should be confident that the slickrock affords good purchase.

Vistas from the start are dramatic and far-reaching, stretching to the Pink Cliffs of the Table Cliff Plateau on the western horizon and far southwest to the Straight Cliffs bounding the Kaiparowits Plateau. Below you the drainage of Calf Creek unfolds, exposing miles of sweeping, cross-bedded, white Navajo slickrock.

Below the first short band of slickrock, a few minor switchbacks ensue, leading through volcanic boulders on a moderately steep grade down to the next band of slickrock. Descend this sandstone slope, aiming for the obvious trail on the flats below. Once you reach this wide, well-worn sandy path, 300 feet below the rim, you begin a gradual descent over the sandy, gently sloping bench.

Seasonal wildflowers splash their colors across the trailside slopes. Look for the white blooms of cryptantha and evening primrose, the yellow blossoms of goldenweed, and the delicate, lilylike, purple blooms of spiderwort.

As you approach the inner gorge of Calf Creek, the trail crosses slickrock once again, where ponderosa pines make an occasional appearance among the woodland trees. Soon the cottonwood and Gambel oak groves in the canyon bottom come into view, and as you reach the rim of the inner gorge, the trail turns right and leads upcanyon. By now you can hear the echo of the waterfall, but you cannot yet see it.

Soon the trail splits: The lower trail to the left descends over slickrock to the foot of the falls, and the upper trail to the right continues upcanyon to the head of the falls. Following the upper trail above the gorge, a lovely pool comes into view below, and behind it, a deep alcove rich with hanging-garden vegetation. Then another pool, deeper and larger, appears, and finally the falls are before you, an impressive veil of white water plunging about 50 feet over a sandstone precipice.

The trail leads to a small pool at the top of the falls, where Calf Creek's banks are fringed with a ribbon of willow, water birch, and silver buffaloberry. Scattered cottonwoods and ponderosa pines also occur in the canyon bottom, while slickrock slopes flank either side of the perennial stream. Just above the falls is a chain of small pools and deep water pockets, irresistible on a hot day.

The lower trail descends slickrock, where there may be cairns to lead the way, for several hundred yards to a shady alcove at the foot of the falls. Beware of the abundant poison ivy here, which grows 3 to 4 feet tall and is recognizable by its woody stem and large shiny green leaves, growing in sets of three. Here the music of the falls is enjoyed to its best advantage, and the large pool below is an added bonus on a hot day.

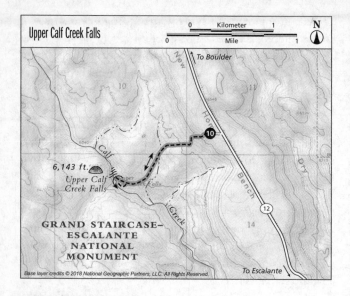

Miles and Directions

0.0 Begin hiking at the trailhead register.

1.0 Reach the small pool at the top of Upper Calf Creek Falls.
Return by the same route.

2.0 Arrive back at the trailhead.

11 Lower Calf Creek Falls

This trip is one of the premier day hikes in the Escalante region, and for good reasons. The excellent self-guiding nature trail is easily accessible from the scenic UT 12. In addition, a pleasant campground located at the trailhead, a spectacular cliff-bound canyon, a perennial stream featuring beaver ponds and abundant trout, and a memorable veil of white water—one of very few active waterfalls in the southern Utah desert—plunging into a cold, deep pool combine to make this trip a must for any hiker visiting the region.

Distance: 6.2 miles round-trip

Hiking time: 3.5–4 hours

Difficulty: Easy

Trail surface: Good constructed trail, moderately sandy in places

Best season: Mar through June; Sept through Oct

Canine compatibility: Leashed dogs permitted

Water availability: Available at the picnic site at the trailhead from spring through fall. Calf Creek—treat before drinking, or bring your own.

Hazards: Negligible

Permits: Not required

Maps: *USGS Calf Creek* (trail not shown on quad); *Trails Illustrated Canyons of the Escalante*

Finding the trailhead: The prominently signed BLM Calf Creek Recreation Area is located off UT 12, 11.4 miles south of the UT 12/Burr Trail Road junction in Boulder, 14.4 miles northeast of Escalante, and 1.1 miles north of the Escalante River Bridge on UT 12. Follow the paved spur road for about 250 yards below the highway to the day-use parking lot. A small day-use fee is collected by campground hosts at the entrance to the parking lot.

The Hike

From the day-use parking area adjacent to the picnic site, follow the paved road north through the campground for 0.2 mile, following signs pointing to the trail. Just before the road dips down to ford Calf Creek, the prominently signed trail heads left up the west slopes of the canyon.

As you proceed, refer to the brochure provided by the campground hosts as you entered the recreation area. It is keyed to fifteen numbered posts along the trail, pointing out the vegetation and geologic features at each and describing the area's history and prehistory. The brochure will greatly enhance your appreciation and enjoyment of the area.

The wide, sometimes rocky, and often sandy trail winds upcanyon along the west slopes above Calf Creek, passing through fields of rabbitbrush, groves of Gambel oak, and woodlands of pinyon and juniper, which provide occasional shade. An active beaver population has felled most of the cottonwoods along the grass-bordered creek, but they have ignored the abundant water birch fringing the streamside.

After about 2 miles, you reach the banks of Calf Creek for the first time, and the canyon floor ahead grows increasingly narrow. Box elders, water birches, and Gambel oaks mass their ranks on the canyon bottom and on the shady slopes just above. Now you can gaze into the clear waters of Calf Creek, brimming with fat brook trout reaching 12 inches in length, a rare sight in a desert canyon. The contrast here between the luxuriant riparian greenery and the stark profile of sandstone cliffs and domes is dramatic.

As you pass a chain of large beaver ponds, you can hear the echoing crash of the waterfall long before you see it. Suddenly, you round a bend and the falls appear. Soon thereafter you reach the trail's end in the confines of a slickrock amphitheater.

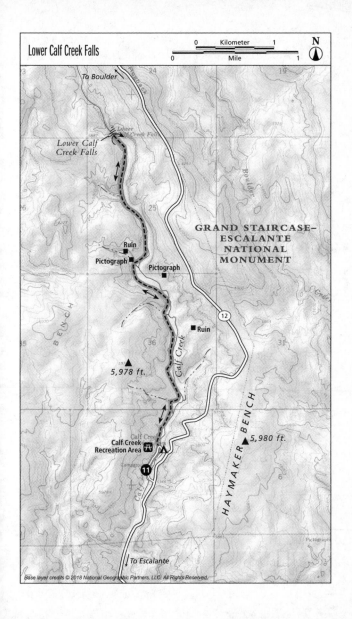

Lower Calf Creek Falls

To Boulder

Lower Calf
Creek Falls

Ruin
Pictograph
Pictograph

GRAND STAIRCASE–
ESCALANTE
NATIONAL
MONUMENT

Ruin

12

▲ 5,978 ft.

Calf Creek

▲ 5,980 ft.

HAYMAKER BENCH

Calf Creek
Recreation Area

11

To Escalante

0   Kilometer   1

0   Mile   1

N

The memorable 126-foot waterfall plunges in one leap over the sandstone precipice above, then thunders onto a moss-draped slickrock wall and spreads a veil of white water into the deep green pool below. From the walls of the amphitheater issue an array of dripping springs that nurture hanging gardens of maidenhair fern and alcove columbine. Here you can relax in a shady grove of water birch or cool off in the deep pool in the spray of the falls.

Bear in mind that Lower Calf Creek is a day-use area only—no overnight backpacking is allowed along the trail. Camp only in the Calf Creek Campground at the trailhead.

Miles and Directions

0.0 From the day-use parking area, follow the paved road north through the campground.

0.2 Just before the road crosses Calf Creek, you will see signs pointing out the trail on the left (northwest) side of the road. Turn left and follow the obvious trail.

3.1 Reach the base of Lower Calf Creek Falls. Return the way you came.

6.2 Arrive back at the trailhead.

12 Devils Garden

The Devils Garden Outstanding Natural Area is an excellent place off Hole-in-the-Rock Road for an afternoon picnic followed by an hour or so of rewarding exploration. The garden is small, covering only about 200 acres, but it is a miniature wonderland of Navajo Sandstone hoodoos, domes, narrow passages, and small arches, hidden from the view of drivers along Hole-in-the-Rock Road.

Distance: Variable, up to 0.7 mile

Hiking time: Variable, up to 1 hour

Difficulty: Easy

Trail surface: Boot-worn trails and slickrock routes

Best season: Apr through early June; Sept through Oct

Canine compatibility: Leashed dogs permitted

Water availability: Bring your own.

Hazards: Negligible

Permits: Not required

Maps: *USGS Seep Flat; Trails Illustrated Canyons of the Escalante*

Finding the trailhead: The prominently signed Hole-in-the-Rock Road, a BLM Scenic Backway, branches southeast from UT 12, 5.8 miles east of the Escalante Interagency Visitor Center in Escalante and 23.8 miles southwest of the UT 12/Burr Road junction in Boulder. Follow the good, wide, graded road southeast, passing a large destination and mileage sign a short distance from the highway. After driving 10.5 miles from the highway, you pass the signed turnoff to Harris Wash trailhead. Continue south on Hole-in-the-Rock Road for another 1.6 miles (12.1 miles from UT 12) to the signed spur road leading to Devils Garden, and turn right. Follow this gravel road for 0.25 mile to the spacious parking area adjacent to the picnic site.

The Hike

Devils Garden provides a brief introduction to the kind of slickrock walking and route-finding over a trailless landscape typical of most backcountry routes in the Escalante region. Since landscape features such as pour-offs and cliffs are in miniature here, obstacles are minor.

Devils Garden features a four-site picnic area with pit toilets, tables, fire pits, and elevated grills. No water is available. Also, bring your own firewood or charcoal, since firewood collecting is not allowed at the site. Dogs must be leashed at all times in Devils Garden. Although children will enjoy wandering with their parents here, remind your kids to avoid trampling the coarse yet fragile desert vegetation.

There is no particular destination other than the garden itself, and there are numerous short, boot-worn paths to follow. Or you can strike out on your own over the slickrock. Since everything here is on a small scale, it's easy to experience the entire area by wandering through it for an hour or so.

Miniature domes, tiny narrows carved by rivulets of infrequent runoff, and diminutive pour-offs are among the features you'll see during your wanderings. Mano Arch can be found by following the upper, left-hand trail beginning at the picnic site. The lower trail skirts the base of Devils Garden's erosion formations, passing another delicate arch, an array of red-and-beige-toned sandstone hoodoos, and mushroom rocks that rise from the pinyon-and-juniper-studded bench. Other hiker-made trails crisscross the area.

You can follow a short loop through the garden, covering about 0.7 mile along the way. The upper trail fades on the slickrock past the aforementioned arch, but you can continue over the sandstone slopes to a point above a bend

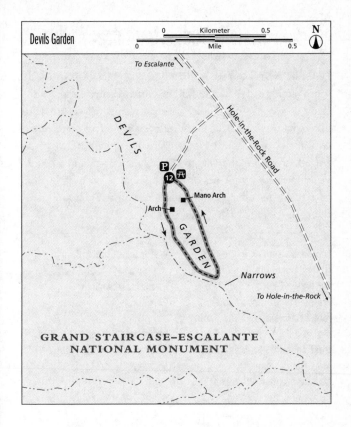

Kilometer

To Escalante

Hole-in-the-Rock Road

D E V I L S

P
12

Mano Arch

Arch

G A R D E N

Narrows

To Hole-in-the-Rock

**GRAND STAIRCASE–ESCALANTE
NATIONAL MONUMENT**

N

0   Kilometer   0.5
0   Mile   0.5

in the wash, where it cuts through a 15-foot-wide slot. Loop back to the picnic site via the bench above the wash, skirting the dramatic hoodoos along the garden's western margin. Midway back to the picnic site, you'll pick up a good trail to follow back to your car.

13   Fortymile Ridge to Sunset Arch

Few hikers visit Sunset Arch, a delicate, graceful span on the south slopes of Fortymile Ridge, which is surprising considering the arch is accessible via a short and easy route. Most hikers who come to Fortymile Ridge are en route to one of two access routes into famous Coyote Gulch, north of the ridge. Vistas along the way to the arch are far-ranging, and the walking is easy, with no obstacles. There is no trail, but one isn't really necessary along this straightforward route across the open terrain.

Distance: 3 miles round-trip
Hiking time: 1–1.5 hours
Difficulty: Easy
Trail surface: Cross-country route; rudimentary route-finding required
Best season: Mid-Mar through May; Sept through Oct
Canine compatibility: Leashed dogs permitted

Water availability: Bring your own.
Hazards: Negligible
Permits: Not required for day hiking
Maps: *USGS King Mesa; Trails Illustrated Canyons of the Escalante*

Finding the trailhead: Follow Hole-in-the-Rock Road south from UT 12 for 33.8 miles to Hurricane Wash. Continue south for another 2.2 miles to the signed turnoff to Fortymile Ridge, then turn left (northeast). This narrow, sandy road typically develops a severe washboard surface along its entire course, which undulates over the shrub-dotted, sandy expanse of Fortymile Ridge. The openness of the terrain affords inspiring vistas into the slickrock labyrinths of Coyote Gulch and the lower Escalante canyons and to the more distant landmarks of the Aquarius Plateau, Straight Cliffs, Navajo Mountain, and the Henry Mountains.

After 4.3 miles, turn left (north) onto a short, but steep and rough, spur road leading 0.1 mile to a large steel water tank and parking area atop the ridge. There are a few pullouts used as camping areas along Fortymile Ridge Road and many more undeveloped campsites along the course of Hole-in-the-Rock Road.

The Hike

From the hilltop trailhead at the water tank, drop back down to Fortymile Ridge Road and turn left (northeast), walking another 0.1 mile to a right-angle bend in the road. Leave the road here where you see a small steel water tank and concrete cistern, and follow a southeast course across the gentle, sandy expanse of Fortymile Ridge, heading toward prominent Point 4772 and its red slickrock slopes.

After about ten minutes and 0.3 mile of weaving a course among blackbrush, sand sagebrush, Mormon tea, and silvery sophora, you reach a minor drainage at the foot of Point 4772. Simply follow the drainage generally south and downhill. Broad vistas reach to the bold barrier of the Straight Cliffs and to the broad dome of 10,388-foot Navajo Mountain. Prominent features at the base of the Straight Cliffs include the isolated slickrock domes of the Sooner Rocks, and to the northwest of those domes you see an apron of Entrada sandstone at the foot of Cave Point, where an array of deep alcoves create an intriguing contrast of light and shadow.

The better route ahead skirts the shallow arroyo of the drainage rather than following its winding course. The left (east) side of the arroyo is much less sandy than the right side. After about 1 mile the arroyo ends when you reach an expanse of Navajo Sandstone slickrock. Using the distant Sooner Rocks as your guide, continue on your southbound course. Traverse the rolling slickrock for about five minutes, and suddenly Sunset Arch appears on the low rim just ahead.

Angle upward to the small arch, relax in its shade, and soak in the tremendous panorama. Sunset is a small arch— about 10 feet high and stretching perhaps 50 feet between abutments—but it is a thin, graceful span, created by the eroded remnants of a dome of iron-rich Navajo Sandstone. A few past visitors, some as early as 1924, have left inscriptions in the arch. Please restrain the urge to leave your own mark behind.

True to its name, the arch faces west and frames a memorable sunset over the Straight Cliffs. Views reach south across the vast terrace traversed by Hole-in-the-Rock Road, a landscape little changed since the members of the epic Hole-in-the-Rock Expedition pioneered the route in 1879 and 1880.

About 0.25 mile away, across the draw below to the southeast, you can see another small arch piercing a low dome of Navajo Sandstone.

From Sunset Arch, retrace your route to the trailhead.

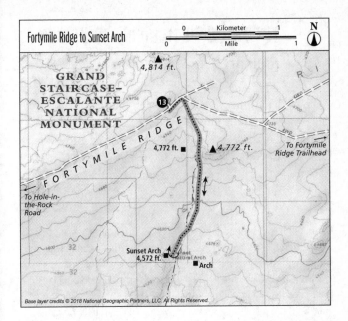

Miles and Directions

0.0   Begin hiking at the trailhead parking area near the water tank. Follow the spur road back to Fortymile Ridge Road.

0.1   Turn left (northeast) onto Fortymile Ridge Road.

0.2   Leave the road at a right-angle curve, next to a small water tank and concrete cistern, and bear right (southeast) toward Point 4772. At the foot of Point 4772, drop into the drainage and continue in a generally south direction.

1.0   As the drainage ends and slickrock route begins, use Sooner Rocks as your guide to continue heading south. Keep an eye out for cairns to guide your way.

1.5   Reach Sunset Arch. Turn around and head back to the trailhead.

3.0   Arrive back at the trailhead.

14 Willow Gulch Trailhead to Broken Bow Arch

Willow Gulch offers one of the best short day hikes, also suitable as an overnight trip, in the lower Escalante canyons. The scenic route follows slickrock gorges sliced into a domed landscape of Navajo Sandstone. Interesting narrow passages, a ribbon of riparian foliage, beaver ponds in the small stream, and the large Broken Bow Arch are major attractions.

Distance: 4 miles round-trip
Hiking time: 2–3 hours
Difficulty: Easy
Trail surface: Wash route
Best season: Mid-Mar through May; Sept through Oct
Canine compatibility: Leashed dogs permitted
Water availability: Intermittent flows below confluence with Willow Gulch after 1 mile; treat before drinking or bring your own.
Hazards: Flash flood danger
Permits: Not required for day hikes
Maps: *USGS Sooner Bench* and *Davis Gulch; Trails Illustrated Canyons of the Escalante*

Finding the trailhead: Follow Hole-in-the-Rock Road for 36 miles southeast from UT 12 to Fortymile Ridge Road, and continue straight ahead, soon passing historic Dance Hall Rock. The road ahead undulates through several shallow drainages and is often rocky, rough, and at times steep and winding.

You pass the signed left turn to Fortymile Spring (the site of one of the Hole-in-the-Rock expedition's camps during the winter of 1879–1880) at 37.5 miles, cross Carcass Wash at 39.4 miles, and, finally, cross Sooner Wash at 40.5 miles. Several spur roads just beyond Sooner Wash lead to excellent undeveloped campsites among the Entrada sandstone domes of the Sooner Rocks.

An unsigned road branches left (east) 1 mile beyond Sooner Wash, atop the desert terrace of Sooner Bench. Turn left here and follow the narrow track east. This road, which is occasionally rocky with washboards in places, is passable to 4WD vehicles and carefully driven 2WD vehicles. You will enter Glen Canyon National Recreation Area after 0.6 mile and reach the trailhead at the road end after 1.4 miles, 42.9 miles from UT 12.

The Hike

A well-worn path begins behind the trailhead register, descending a moderate grade down the sandy slope. The beautiful canyon, embraced by desert-varnished walls of Navajo Sandstone, opens up 150 feet below. Within moments you pass an interesting slab-crowned hoodoo, then bend east and descend slickrock and sand into the broad wash below. An intriguing stretch of narrows lies a short distance upcanyon, where the wash boxes up in an alcove decorated with hanging gardens. Once you reach the canyon floor, follow the sandy wash downcanyon, shortly passing a line of seepage fringed with the delicate fronds of maidenhair fern.

Soon the wash slots up, and most hikers bypass this slot by following a path above, on the right (south) side of the drainage. The wash opens up again beyond that first constriction, but soon you are funneled into a passable stretch of narrows, beyond which the mouth of a prominent side canyon opens up on the right after 0.5 mile, while on the left, a smaller draw joins the wash.

Continue straight ahead down the narrow, sandy stone hallway. The contrast between the cross-bedded, salmon-tinted slickrock above and the verdant riparian foliage is dramatic. Soon a pair of paths begins following benches on either side of the wash as you approach the confluence with Willow Gulch, which joins on the right after 0.9 mile among tall Fremont cottonwoods. Turn left and now follow Willow Gulch downcanyon. Water soon begins to flow in the wash, and evidence of beaver activity attests to its reliability. Willow Gulch opens up below the confluence, with grassy, brush-studded benches flanking the wash and sheer desert-varnished cliffs and domes of Navajo Sandstone rising above. The canyon, however, remains fairly shallow. Rarely do the domes atop the rim rise more than 200 feet from the canyon floor.

After walking for several minutes below the confluence, a prominent trail forged by hikers trying to avoid wading in the stream leads you up onto the right-hand bench. At length the bench pinches out and you descend a minor gully back into the wash, where you jump across the stream and follow a trail on the north-side bench, skirting a beaver pond. Shortly you return to the wash, where the canyon grows increasingly narrow, bounded by bold cliffs and domes. Follow the twists and turns of the wash ahead, repeatedly crossing the small stream and tracing bypass trails above it. The stream is small but maintains a steady flow, periodically widening into pools and scooped-out water pockets. Expect minor bushwhacking on occasion through thickets of limber willow and stiff tamarisk.

After curving around a prominent bend in the canyon, the large Broken Bow Arch suddenly appears ahead. Cross the stream and follow the obvious trail up to the bench opposite the arch. The creek flows beneath a low overhang just below the bench, but a screen of Gambel oaks hides most of the streambed from view. From the bench, look for a steep, sandy trail that drops into the oak grove below. Do not continue following the trail on the bench, as other hikers have, since it dead-ends at an overhang and you'll have to backtrack.

You regain the wash where an overhanging ledge, the topmost layer of Kayenta Formation rocks, shades the stream and hanging gardens of maidenhair fern directly below the arch. From here you can turn left, upstream, and scramble up to the arch, or continue downcanyon and approach the arch from the opposite side. Follow the base of the overhang a short distance ahead to a bend in the canyon. A boot-worn path leaves the wash at the bend on the north side. Follow the path up to the bench, then head northwest the short distance up to the arch.

Piercing a thick fin of Navajo Sandstone that projects into the canyon from the north wall, the huge triangle-shaped aperture of Broken Bow Arch frames a memorable view of the convoluted canyon walls beyond. The base of the opening is heaped with great angular boulders, which fell from above as stress fractures inexorably enlarged the span. The arch is shaded with a rich brown patina of desert varnish. Tall, spreading cottonwoods in the wash below add a delicate contrast to the scene.

From Broken Bow Arch, retrace your steps to return to the trailhead.

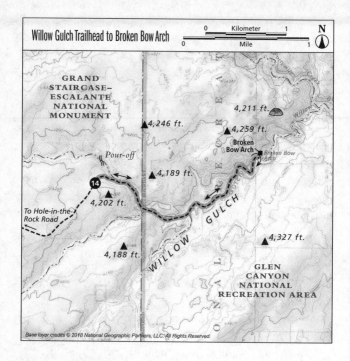

Miles and Directions

0.0   Begin hiking at the trailhead register and follow the trail down the sandy slope.

0.2   Enter the wash.

0.9   Come to the confluence with Willow Gulch. Turn left and follow Willow Gulch downcanyon.

2.0   Reach Broken Bow Arch. Turn around and return the way you came.

4.0   Arrive back at the trailhead.

Grand Staircase– Paria Canyon

T he aptly named Grand Staircase marches northward like a series of Brobdingnagian stairs, from the Arizona Strip to the 9,000-foot edge of Utah's High Plateaus. The colorful succession of "risers" in the staircase include, from south to north, the Shinarump Cliffs, the Vermilion Cliffs, the White Cliffs, the Gray Cliffs, and, finally, the Pink Cliffs. Progressively higher terraces separate each cliff band, and all together this cliff and terrace landscape is remarkably uniform and quite unique. The Grand Staircase can be best viewed from a scenic overlook off US 89, between Fredonia and Jacob Lake, Arizona. From that vantage, the landscape to the north in Utah indeed resembles a staircase, and for people inclined toward hiking and/or scenic driving, it is an alluring scene.

The Grand Staircase is the most remote, seldom-visited section of the Glen Canyon region covered in this book, though it is spectacular and contains the most extensive network of slot canyons in Utah. By way of contrast, the Paria Canyon–Vermilion Cliffs Wilderness, at the southwest corner of the Glen Canyon region, is so popular that annual visitation there almost outnumbers all other hiking areas in the region combined.

Comparable to other regions covered in this book, hiking in the Grand Staircase–Paria Canyon region is most often achieved without the benefit of a trail. Most of the easy day hikes follow dry, easily passable washes, leading through some of the finest narrows in the region. The exception is the excellent Panorama Trail in Kodachrome Basin State Park.

Camping

There are four public campgrounds in this region. The twenty-seven-unit campground in Kodachrome Basin State Park is located 2.2 miles north of Cottonwood Canyon Road, 9.4 miles from UT 12 at Cannonville, Utah. This popular, scenic campground is open year-round and provides excellent facilities, for a fee, that include tables, water, fire grills, showers, and a centrally located restroom. The sites and cabins can be reserved online at Reserve America: https://reserveamerica. com/camping/kodachrome-basin-state-park/r/campground Details.do?contractCode=UT&parkId=345501, and several of them can accommodate large trailers and RVs. Unreserved sites are available on a first-come, first-served basis. A camper's store is located at Trailhead Station, next to the Panorama trailhead, 0.5 mile from the campground.

The second campground is located at the White House trailhead, the portal to Paria Canyon, 2 miles below the Paria Contact Station. Pay the appropriate fees and register for your stay in the campground at the information kiosk just off the highway, immediately below the Paria Contact Station, then drive 2 miles down the bumpy dirt road to the campground and trailhead. White House has five small walk-in sites, used primarily by Paria Canyon hikers. Its facilities include tables, fire grills, and pit toilets. You must pack out all your trash. No water is available, and there is a five-person limit at each site. The site is managed by the Kanab Field Office.

The third site is the Lees Ferry Campground below Glen Canyon Dam in Glen Canyon National Recreation Area, available for a fee. This campground, accessed via a paved road, is one of the most scenic sites in the region. The campground rests on a terrace that affords dramatic views of the emerald-green waters of the Colorado River, the 3,000-foot facade of the Vermilion Cliffs, and the crags of the Echo Peaks. Facilities include awnings that shade tables, fire grills, water, toilets, and garbage collection. Lees Ferry has fifty-four sites managed by the National Park Service, which are first come, first served and can be reserved for a small fee per night.

At the Paria Movie Set, located south of Kanab off US 89, there is a small walk-in campground featuring three sites with tables, a barbecue grill and fire pit, and pit toilets. No water is available, and there is no fee. Do not attempt to drive to Paria Movie Set if the road is wet, which makes it impassable and dangerous.

Elsewhere in the region you are free to camp anywhere you wish on BLM-administered public lands, and there is ample opportunity to do so, particularly alongside Cottonwood Canyon and Skutumpah Roads. Please use established camping and parking spaces for car camping, and use extreme caution if building a campfire.

Access and Services

Two scenic highways, UT 12 and US 89, traverse this region from east to west. On the north, UT 12 (the only access to Bryce Canyon National Park) provides a 59-mile scenic link between Escalante and US 89 south of Panguitch, Utah. To the south, US 89 deviates from its usual north-to-south route and leads east and west for 71 miles between Kanab, Utah, and Page, Arizona.

On the extreme southern fringes of the region, mostly in Arizona, US 89A, yet another scenic route, is a 91-mile highway linking Kanab with US 89, 23 miles south of Page and 100 miles north of Flagstaff. This highway, the only way to reach the North Rim of the Grand Canyon, provides access to Lees Ferry at the mouth of the Paria River.

Linking UT 12 in the north with US 89 in the south are two long, remote, and graded dirt roads: Cottonwood Canyon Road and Skutumpah Road. Of these two routes, among the most scenic drives in Grand Staircase–Escalante National Monument, Skutumpah Road receives more frequent maintenance and is the better road. Cottonwood Canyon Road is subject to washouts and can be severely damaged by runoff from heavy rains. The road should be avoided in wet weather, when even minor rainfall renders its bentonite clay surface impassable. Before driving either road, obtain an updated road report from the Kanab BLM office, the Paria Contact Station on US 89 between Kanab and Page, or the Escalante Interagency Visitor Center in Escalante.

Both roads begin in Cannonville, on UT 12 in Bryce Valley, 23 miles east of US 89 (10 miles south of Panguitch) and 36 miles west of Escalante. Cottonwood Canyon Road (of which the first 7.2 miles are paved) stretches 46 miles from UT 12 to US 89, 26 miles west of Page. Skutumpah Road leads 52 miles to US 89, 8 miles east of Kanab.

Kanab and Page are your best sources for whatever you may need while traveling through the region. Both towns offer a full range of services. On the north, the small town of Tropic, Utah, is your only source of supplies between Panguitch and Escalante. Tropic offers motels, gas, car repair and towing, restaurants, and groceries.

The Grand Staircase–Escalante National Monument, Kanab Headquarters, can provide excellent up-to-date information for the area at (435) 644-1200. Or you can visit the office by following signs that point to the way in Kanab. The Paria Contact Station is another excellent source of information if you're traveling between Page and Kanab on US 89.

In the event of an emergency, dial 911 or contact the Kane County Sheriff in Utah at (435) 644-2349. In Arizona, dial 911 for emergencies or contact the Coconino County Sheriff in Flagstaff at (800) 338-7888 or the National Park Service in Page at (800) 582-4351.

15 Kodachrome Basin State Park, Panorama Trail

Kodachrome Basin State Park, a 2,240-acre preserve southeast of Bryce Canyon National Park, is a place of vivid colors and dramatic landforms. Punctuated by the white chimneys of sand pipes, the orange cliffs, spires, and finlike ridges of Entrada sandstone that dominate the basin make it one of the more spectacular areas in southern Utah, a land renowned for its unique landscapes.

Distance: 5.4 miles round-trip
Hiking time: 3–3.5 hours
Difficulty: Moderately easy
Trail surface: 4WD road and constructed trail, well defined
Best season: Apr through early June; Sept through Oct
Canine compatibility: Leashed dogs permitted

Water availability: Bring your own.
Hazards: Negligible
Permits: Not required
Maps: USGS Henrieville and Cannonville (trails and state park not shown on quads; a trail map is available at the visitor center)

Finding the trailhead: From UT 12 in the Bryce Valley town of Cannonville, 33 miles east of Panguitch and US 89, and 36 miles west of Escalante, turn south onto Cottonwood Canyon Road (the Cottonwood Canyon Scenic Backway), signed for Kodachrome Basin–9. Follow this paved road south through Cannonville, then through the broad valley of the upper Paria River. You pass the junction with southwest-bound Skutumpah Road after 2.9 miles, and after 7.4 miles reach the end of pavement on Cottonwood Canyon Road. Turn left here, staying on the paved road, to enter Kodachrome Basin State Park.

Stop at the visitor center after 0.9 mile and pay a small day-use fee, then continue north 0.6 mile to the signed parking area for Panorama Trail, Grand Parade Trail, and the picnic area.

The signed Panorama trailhead is located on the left (west) side of the road, 1.6 miles from Cottonwood Canyon Road and 8.8 miles from Cannonville. The twenty-seven-unit campground is located 0.4 mile from the trailhead, along the loop at the road's end.

The Hike

This state park is like a national park in miniature. Its concentration of unusual landforms, good access, numerous short trails, and visitor services that include a general store, campground, and cabins combine to make the park a premier destination.

Six hiking trails traverse the park, most of them less than 1 mile in length. The exception is the Panorama Trail, a nearly level 2.9-mile loop that surveys what is perhaps the finest scenery the park has to offer. Panorama Point, an overlook just above the loop trail, affords an unparalleled vista across the park's colorful landscape. The 2.5-mile Big Bear Geyser Trail can be taken to extend the trip into a rewarding half-day hike.

Hikers, mountain bikers, and stagecoach tours (conducted by the park concessionaire at Trailhead Station from April through mid-October) share 1 mile of the Panorama Trail. The remaining singletrack is shared by hikers and mountain bikers only. The Panorama Trail and Big Bear Geyser Trail are the only trails open to mountain bikes in the park.

The sand pipes in the park add a unique dimension to a land dominated by unusual landforms. These white, chimney-like spires, averaging 30 to 50 feet in height, are composed of coarse sand that is far more resistant to erosion than the overlying orange Entrada sandstone. Geologists believe that long ago the park was a geothermal area, with hot springs and geysers, much like Yellowstone National Park is today. After the springs and geysers ceased to flow, they filled with sand and are the white spires you see today.

The wide trail, narrower than a typical dirt road, begins behind the trailhead display sign and traverses a grassy flat studded with juniper, big sagebrush, rabbitbrush, and four-wing saltbush. From the start you are surrounded by an array of orange Entrada sandstone spires. Other spires you will see along the trail are the white sand pipes, the resistant sediment-filled cores of ancient geysers and hot springs.

Many of the spires along the trail have been likened to familiar images and given fanciful names. Soon you reach the first, Fred Flintstone Spire, rising from bedrock. Just beyond it the trail forks after 0.3 mile, with the return leg of the loop branching left. Bear right and quite soon you reach the first of several short spur trails. It leads 100 yards to Old Indian Cave, a small, shady alcove. This short loop trail returns to the main trail.

The trail ahead traverses a gently contoured basin covered in grass and studded with the gnarled trees of the pinyon-juniper woodland. Fine views reach west to the Pink Cliffs of the Paunsaugunt Plateau in Bryce Canyon National Park. After 0.6 mile, the stagecoach road branches left, and you follow the singletrack ahead where the sign indicates the Panorama Trail. A tall, slender sand pipe, Ballerina Spire, rises a short distance north of the trail. You curve around it and soon reach the 200-yard spur trail to Hat Shop, a concentration of orange Entrada spires capped by sandstone slabs.

Colorful badlands slopes rise 600 feet above the Hat Shop to the north rim of the basin. The spires here are composed of the orange Gunsight Member of the Entrada Formation;

above, the red Cannonville Member and the white Escalante Member rise in barren, intricately eroded slopes to the rim of Henrieville sandstone.

Beyond the Hat Shop, the trail traverses west across the open basin, bounded ahead to the west and southwest by a trio of large slickrock domes. The gentle trail passes through an open pinyon-juniper woodland, where the flats are dotted with sagebrush and a variety of native bunchgrasses, including Indian ricegrass, needle-and-thread grass, and sand dropseed. As you approach the foot of the northernmost dome, you reach the Secret Passage Trail. This trail branches right, forming a 0.2-mile loop that includes the narrow slot of Secret Passage and a view of White Buffalo, an unusual sand pipe formation perched atop the rim.

A short distance beyond the Secret Passage Trail, you come to the junction with the Big Bear Geyser Trail, branching right 1 mile from the trailhead. Turn right onto that trail, following a brief steep descent off the ridge via badlands slopes. Below, you level off in a wooded basin and skirt the base of intricately eroded 200-foot cliffs. Along this part of the trail, you will capture glimpses into the canyon of the upper Paria River, where it carves a gorge through the White Cliffs (Navajo Sandstone) of the Grand Staircase.

After hiking 0.6 mile from the Panorama Trail, you reach the signed spur trail that branches left, leading 0.1 mile to Mammoth Geyser, the largest sand pipe in the park. Another sand pipe, one of the Big Bear Geysers, is visible on the rim of the cliffs north of the junction, and it can be viewed at a better advantage ahead.

Bear right at that junction, and quite soon you reach another junction, where signs point right and left to the Big Bear Geyser Trail. Taking the right fork, you soon curve into an amphitheater, where a 100-yard spur trail leads to the base of the cliffs atop which Big Bear Geyser rests. The trail ahead briefly becomes indistinct as it follows a small wash to the mouth of a precipitous slot canyon slicing through the cliffs just above. There, atop the rim, is the second geyser, called Mama Bear Geyser.

The trail ahead follows the wash draining the basin until the wash curves east. Avoid the path leading into that east-trending canyon unless you wish to explore it. The main trail bends west here, skirting the cliffs for another 0.2 mile to the Cool Cave spur trail. Hikers won't want to miss this side trip.

The spur trail leads north into a small wash, which you follow up into an increasingly narrow slot. When the slot bends to the right you reach Cool Cave, actually a deep alcove lying beneath a pour-off. Only a small patch of sky is visible overhead as the vaulting cliffs nearly envelop you.

Back on the main trail, the final 0.25 mile of the loop follows a gently undulating course across the basin, affording a longer-range perspective of the Big Bear Geysers. After closing the loop, backtrack for 0.7 mile to the Panorama Trail and turn right.

The Panorama Trail skirts the eastern foot of the first dome, then curves west around it, where the coach road and the trail merge. Just beyond the southern foot of the dome, a short spur trail leads to a fine vista point, where views unfold across the western reaches of Kodachrome Basin, including Mammoth Geyser, with a backdrop of the glowing Pink Cliffs.

Follow the coach road generally south toward Hogan Temple, the bold, convoluted slickrock dome straight ahead. The road soon skirts the second of the three domes, where you reach a signed junction. The coach road continues ahead and quickly ends in a loop. The return leg of the Panorama

Trail branches left. If you wish to reach Panorama Point, turn right and ascend 120 feet in 0.2 mile, via a series of steep switchbacks. The point is actually the apex of a debris cone that mantles the eastern flanks of the dome.

From Panorama Point, Kodachrome Basin spreads out in all its colorful splendor. The basin below the viewpoint, with its velvety grasslands and pinyon-juniper woodlands, adds a soft contrast to the raw, rockbound landscape that surrounds it.

From the junction below Panorama Point, the return trail undulates across the basin for 0.5 mile to the junction, where

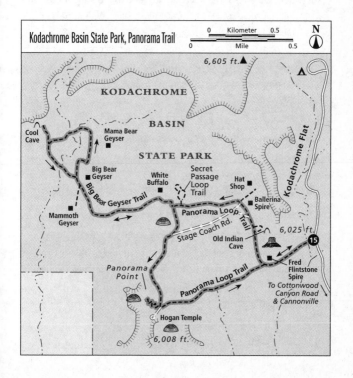

you turn right and backtrack around Fred Flintstone Spire for 0.3 mile to the trailhead.

Miles and Directions

0.0 Begin hiking at the Panorama trailhead.

0.3 Come to the junction with the return leg of the loop trail and bear right.

0.6 The 4WD road branches left; bear right onto the foot trail. Shortly after, you will reach Ballerina Spire, located on the right (north) side of the trail.

0.7 Come to the spur trail leading to Hat Shop. Bear right to visit the Hat Shop, or stay left to continue on Panorama Trail.

1.0 Reach the junction with the Big Bear Geyser Trail; bear right. (Option: For a shorter 2.9-mile loop, turn left [south] and loop back around to the trailhead.)

1.6 Come to a spur trail to Mammoth Geyser on your left (southwest).

1.7 Junction with loop trail; bear right.

2.3 Junction with trail to Cool Cave; turn right.

2.4 Cool Cave.

2.5 Return to the loop trail; turn right.

2.8 End of loop trail; bear right.

3.5 Return to the Panorama Trail; turn right (south).

3.7 Foot trail merges with coach road; continue straight ahead.

4.1 Junction with return leg of the Panorama Loop Trail (left) and Panorama Point Trail; bear right to Panorama Point.

4.3 Reach Panorama Point. Backtrack to return trail and proceed east.

5.1 Loop Trail junction; bear right.

5.4 Arrive back at the trailhead.

16 Cottonwood Canyon Narrows

Cottonwood Creek, an often-dry stream course, has, over the ages, carved a long, deep, and winding canyon through the steeply tilted rock beds of The Cockscomb, ranging from the shadowed confines of narrow slots to a broad, open wash. This fine, short hike leads through the final narrow gorge of Cottonwood Creek before the canyon opens up and begins its long, straight journey to the confluence with the Paria River. The hike leads through the most easily accessible section of narrows along Cottonwood Creek, offering a rewarding scenic diversion for anyone taking a drive down the remote Cottonwood Canyon Road.

Distance: 3 miles round-trip
Hiking time: About 2 hours
Difficulty: Easy
Trail surface: Wash route
Best season: Apr through early June; Sept through Oct
Canine compatibility: Leashed dogs permitted

Water availability: Bring your own.
Hazards: Flash flood danger
Permits: Not required
Maps: *USGS Butler Valley; BLM Smoky Mountain*

Finding the trailhead: From UT 12 in the town of Cannonville, 33 miles east of Panguitch and US 89, and 36 miles west of Escalante, turn south onto Cottonwood Canyon Road, signed for Kodachrome Basin-9. Follow this paved road south through Cannonville, then through the broad valley of the upper Paria River. You pass the junction with southwest-bound Skutumpah Road after 2.9 miles, and after 7.4 miles reach the end of pavement on Cottonwood Canyon Road.

Continue straight ahead on the graded dirt surface of Cottonwood Canyon Road, which is infrequently maintained and subject to washouts. Throughout much of its course, this undulating, winding road traverses bentonite clay, which, when wet, can become impassable and at best is very dangerous to drive on. A high-clearance vehicle, preferably with 4WD, is recommended, though not required unless runoff has damaged the road.

After 1.5 miles, avoid a left-branching ranch road, and soon thereafter dip into the wash of Rock Springs Creek, fording its shallow stream. Enter Grand Staircase–Escalante National Monument, 4.9 miles from the pavement, then ascend a steep grade to a saddle at 5.8 miles. Avoid the left-branching graded road immediately beyond the cattle guard at the saddle, and continue straight ahead.

A very steep grade soon leads down to the crossing of Round Valley Draw at 7.6 miles. You reach the junction with the signed left fork to Grosvenor Arch after 8.5 miles (15.7 miles from Cannonville). Few travelers forgo the 2-mile round-trip drive to that unique arch and picnic site.

Continuing south on Cottonwood Canyon Road, you soon begin following The Cockscomb. The road crests a saddle 13 miles from the pavement, then begins an exceedingly steep downgrade into the drainage below. En route you can see the road cresting another prominent saddle 0.4 mile to the south. Between the two saddles at the bottom of the grade, the small portal of Cottonwood Canyon Narrows opens up through The Cockscomb just west of the road. A small pullout on the left (east) side of the road affords the only available parking, 0.25 mile south of the north saddle, 250 yards north of the south saddle, and 20.5 miles from Cannonville. Another short spur road branches right 0.9 mile ahead, offering access into the mouth of the narrows.

The trailhead can also be reached from US 89 in the south. Find the southern end of Cottonwood Canyon Road (between mileposts 17 and 18) 2.2 miles east of the Paria Contact Station or 26.3 miles west of Page, Arizona. The turnoff is indicated by a large BLM destination and mileage sign pointing to Cottonwood Canyon, Grosvenor Arch, and Cannonville.

As the road leads north away from US 89, it is sandy at first as it ascends over The Rimrocks. The road passes the Grand Staircase-Escalante National Monument boundary after 1.4 miles, then skirts the dramatic gray shale badlands at the foot of the Kaiparowits Plateau. After curving northwest to the broad valley of the Paria River, the road then begins to ascend the course of Cottonwood Wash.

After 14.1 miles, a dirt road branches right (east) to ascend The Cockscomb. Continue north along Cottonwood Wash for another 11.4 miles to the aforementioned trailhead, 25.5 miles from US 89.

The Hike

The Cottonwood Canyon Scenic Backway is perhaps the premier scenic drive in Grand Staircase–Escalante National Monument. Not only does the road afford access to well-known features such as Kodachrome Basin State Park and the incomparable Grosvenor Arch, it also follows The Cockscomb for many miles, one of the most unusual landforms in the monument.

Opposite the small parking area, you will find a brown BLM post on the boundary of the 136,322-acre Paria-Hackberry Wilderness Study Area. From there a path leads into the narrow wash just below, at the portal to the Cottonwood Canyon Narrows. There are three ways to enter: (1) follow the small wash for 50 yards down to an 8-foot pour-off, which requires one Class 4 move to get up or down; (2) just to the right (north) of the pour-off, follow the steep, rocky path that descends briefly into the wash; or (3) follow the shallow draw located about 100 yards north of the parking area, which offers easy, trouble-free access into Cottonwood Creek.

Once you reach the wash of Cottonwood Creek, you may choose to turn right and explore the slot upcanyon. Chockstones and boulders make travel there challenging, and muddy pools persist in the gorge long after significant rainfall. Heading downcanyon, the walking is easy and passable to any hiker.

From the portal, the canyon bends west, briefly opening up. Soon thereafter, the canyon walls close in and you weave a way down the sandy, occasionally rock-strewn wash. Navajo Sandstone cliffs embrace the gorge, standing 10 to 20 feet apart and rising 200 to 300 feet above. The canyon walls are often sheer, in places overhanging, but fractures and ledges support a scattering of shrubs. Gnarled pinyons and junipers fringe the rims above.

Two precipitous slot canyons join Cottonwood Creek on the right, one ending in a shadowed amphitheater at 0.5 mile, the other at 1 mile. About midway through the narrows, an array of spires looms above on the western rim, and the gorge has reached a depth of 400 to 500 feet. After about 0.8 mile, you reach a prominent keyhole-shaped alcove scooped out of the right-side wall. As you approach the lower reaches of the narrows, the canyon begins to open up and sandy benches appear. In response to increased sunlight and more available space, there is a marked increase in vegetation in this part of the canyon.

Near the end of the canyon, the wash describes a prominent bend to the east, and a small arch becomes visible high on the flanks of Dome 5961 on your left. Soon several more skyline arches appear on the splintered canyon rim ahead to the southeast.

When the canyon bends east, it cuts through the steeply tilted Navajo Sandstone of The Cockscomb, and once again

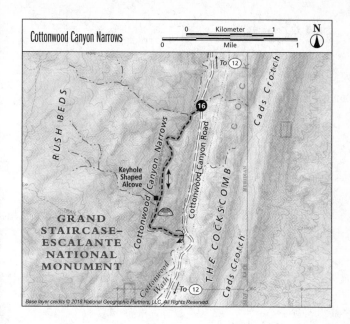

you enter a narrow stone hallway. A boulder jam soon blocks the wash ahead, but there is an easy rock-strewn bypass route on the left side. Beyond that obstacle you exit the gorge and enter an open wash flanked by low benches clad in pinyon-juniper woodland.

Don't be lured too far down the wash. When it bends south, you'll see a pair of cottonwood trees just ahead. Leave the wash there and angle up to the left, soon following a path that quickly leads you to the short spur off of Cottonwood Canyon Road. That spur offers an alternative starting point for a hike into the narrows.

From the road you can return the way you came, or turn left and walk the road for 0.9 mile back to your car.

Miles and Directions

0.0 Begin hiking at the trailhead.

0.8 Reach a keyhole-shaped alcove.

1.5 Reach the mouth of the narrows at Cottonwood Canyon Road. Return by the same route.

3.0 Arrive back at the trailhead.

17 Willis Creek Narrows

On this fine, short hike, there is no particular destination other than the narrows of Willis Creek. Go as far as you wish; the best narrows are found along the first 1.3 miles. Where the broad wash of Willis Creek crosses Skutumpah Road, there is little intimation of the narrow gorge below.

Distance: 4.8 miles round-trip
Hiking time: About 2.5 hours
Difficulty: Easy
Trail surface: Wash route
Best season: Apr through mid-June; Sept through Oct
Canine compatibility: Dogs permitted

Water availability: Seasonal intermittent flows in Willis Creek and Sheep Creek; treat before drinking, or bring your own.
Hazards: Flash flood danger
Permits: Not required
Maps: USGS Bull Valley Gorge; BLM Kanab

Finding the trailhead: From UT 12 in the Bryce Valley town of Cannonville, 33 miles east of Panguitch and US 89, and 36 miles west of Escalante, turn south onto Cottonwood Canyon Road, signed for Kodachrome Basin–9. Follow the pavement through Cannonville, then through the broad valley of the upper Paria River. After 2.9 miles, Skutumpah Road branches right (southwest), signed for Bull Valley Gorge–9 and Kanab–61.

After turning right onto this road, the road immediately dips down to cross the Yellow Creek wash, then rises to the boundary of Grand Staircase–Escalante National Monument after 0.25 mile. After 3 miles, you cross runoff below the spillway of a dam spanning broad Sheep Creek wash, ascend to a ridge, then drop down to the dry wash of Averett Canyon after 4.7 miles. After 5.5 miles, avoid a graded road that branches right near the crest of a ridge. Bear left there and descend to the wash of Willis Creek, 6.3 miles from

Cottonwood Canyon Road. Parking is available on either side of the wash.

The trailhead is also accessible from US 89 in the south. From US 89, turn north where a sign indicates Johnson Canyon, immediately east of milepost 55 and 8 miles east of Kanab, Utah, or 64 miles west of Page, Arizona. Follow this paved road as it gradually ascends Johnson Canyon for 16.2 miles to a signed junction. At the junction, turn right onto the good gravel road (Skutumpah Road), signed for Deer Springs Ranch and Cannonville.

After driving 11.5 miles from the junction, avoid several prominently signed spur roads leading to the private property of Deer Springs Ranch. You reach the Willis Creek wash 26.5 miles from the pavement and 42.7 miles from US 89.

Drivers approaching from either direction will find numerous undeveloped campsites in the pinyon-juniper woodland, many with fine views of the Pink Cliffs of Bryce Canyon National Park.

The Hike

Some of the most dramatic slot canyons in the world have been carved into the White Cliffs of the Grand Staircase in southern Utah. Many of these slot canyons are only accessible to veteran canyoneers well versed in a variety of rock-climbing techniques.

Yet there are slot canyons that involve no more than a pleasant walk down their shadowed stone hallways. Willis Creek is such a canyon. Born on the flanks of the Pink Cliffs in Bryce Canyon National Park, the broad wash of Willis Creek carves a swath through densely wooded terraces until it reaches the Navajo Sandstone of the White Cliffs. There the wash seems to disappear, becoming entrenched between 200- to 300-foot slickrock walls. This gorge, with many narrow passages, stretches 2.5 miles down to its confluence with the much larger Sheep Creek Canyon, another Pink Cliffs drainage.

Cross the road and follow the wash downstream. Soon the Navajo Sandstone emerges and the wash immediately slots up. Scramble down into the wash just below a low pour-off and proceed downcanyon.

At first the Navajo cliffs are low but confining. The occasional appearance of ponderosa pines allows you to judge the height of the canyon walls. After following a few bends of the developing canyon, the walls suddenly rise higher, and you are funneled into a slot where only 6 to 10 feet of space separate the slickrock walls. Although there may be a very small, shallow stream in the upper reaches of the gorge during early spring or following extended periods of rainfall, most of the hike passes over the dry gravel wash.

The canyon beyond the first narrows is variable, ranging from short, narrow slots to more open stretches where benches flank the wash, providing habitat for pinyon pine, juniper, Gambel oak, Rocky Mountain maple, Utah service-berry, seep-willow, alder leaf mountain mahogany, single-leaf ash, and occasional ponderosa pine trees. Within the narrows, only a sliver of sky is visible overhead, where the vaulting walls seem to nearly coalesce. The convoluted slickrock walls, sculpted by ages of abrasive runoff, echo with your footsteps.

After 0.6 mile, you reach another pour-off, easily bypassed via the slickrock ledge on the left side. The drainage of Averett Canyon, entering on the left via a rugged gorge, opens up after 1.3 miles. This canyon was named in honor of Elijah Averett, a member of a party of Utah Territorial Militia in search of Indian raiders who killed settlers in Long Valley, near the town of Glendale, in the spring of 1866. Averett

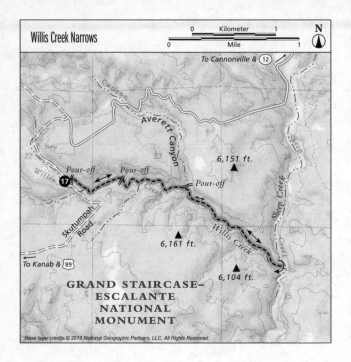

Kilometer

Mile

N

To Cannonville & (12)

Averett Canyon

Canyon

6,151 ft. ▲

Willis

Pour-off   Pour-off

17

Pour-off

Sheep Creek

Skutumpah Road

Willis Creek

Sheep Creek

6,161 ft. ▲

To Kanab & (89)

6,104 ft. ▲

GRAND STAIRCASE–
ESCALANTE
NATIONAL
MONUMENT

himself was killed by Indian rifles in August 1866 while crossing the canyon that now bears his name.

There are no more slots below Averett Canyon—though Willis Creek remains a confined, spectacular canyon—and the walking is easy over the wide gravel wash. When you see a 200-foot cliff apparently blocking your way ahead, you are only minutes away from the confluence with the Sheep Creek wash. From Sheep Creek at 2.4 miles, backtrack through the shadowed gorge to the trailhead.

Miles and Directions

0.0 From the road, hike east into the Willis Creek wash.

1.3 Averett Canyon joins on the left (north) and the narrows end.

2.4 Reach the confluence with Sheep Creek. Return the way you came.

4.8 Arrive back at the trailhead.

18 Lick Wash

Lick Wash is one of many largely unknown, uncelebrated canyons carved into the remote White Cliffs of the Grand Staircase in southern Utah. What Lick Wash lacks in renown is compensated for by its incomparable beauty. Indeed, it is perhaps the most scenic, and seldom-visited, canyon covered in this book. Exciting narrow passages in the upper reaches of the canyon give way to a wider canyon below, embraced by the bold White Cliffs of Navajo Sandstone, rising 600 to 800 feet to the mesa rims above and studded with tall pines. The wash is dry, and travel down its sandy and gravelly bed is easy and passable to any hiker.

Distance: 8 miles round-trip
Hiking time: About 4 hours
Difficulty: Moderately easy
Trail surface: Wash route
Best season: Apr through mid-June; Sept through Oct
Canine compatibility: Dogs permitted

Water availability: Bring your own.
Hazards: Flash flood danger
Permits: Not required
Maps: USGS Deer Spring Point; BLM Kanab

Finding the trailhead: From UT 12 in the Bryce Valley town of Cannonville, 33 miles east of Panguitch and US 89, and 36 miles west of Escalante, turn south onto Cottonwood Canyon Road, signed for Kodachrome Basin–9. Follow the pavement through Cannonville, then through the broad valley of the upper Paria River. After 2.9 miles, Skutumpah Road branches right (southwest), signed for Bull Valley Gorge–9 and Kanab–61.

After turning right onto this road, the road immediately dips down to cross the Yellow Creek wash, then rises to the boundary of Grand Staircase–Escalante National Monument after 0.25 mile. After 3 miles, you cross runoff below the spillway of a dam spanning the broad Sheep Creek wash, ascend to a ridge, then drop down to the dry wash of Averett Canyon after 4.7 miles. After 5.5 miles, avoid a graded road that branches right near the crest of a ridge. Bear left there and descend to the wash of Willis Creek, 6.3 miles from Cottonwood Canyon Road.

Continue straight ahead on Skutumpah Road. After 10.9 miles the road crosses the narrow bridge spanning cavernous Bull Valley Gorge. Enter the signed Bullrush Hollow after 16.9 miles and enjoy the first good views of the towering White Cliffs in the southern distance. After emerging from the woodland at 18.6 miles, you enter the broad, brushy basin of Dry Valley, then gradually descend to an unsigned crossing of Lick Wash at 19.9 miles, where the road is subject to washouts. A short distance beyond the wash, immediately before reaching a cattle guard, turn left onto a faint spur road. Follow the spur for 0.1 mile to its end above the banks of Lick Wash and park there.

From US 89 in the south, you can find the trailhead by turning north where a sign indicates Johnson Canyon. This turnoff is located immediately east of milepost 55 and 8 miles east of Kanab, Utah, or 64 miles west of Page, Arizona. Follow the paved Johnson Canyon Road north for 16.2 miles to a signed junction, then turn right onto the good gravel Skutumpah Road, signed for Deer Springs Ranch and Cannonville.

Avoid several signed spur roads leading to the private property of the Deer Springs Ranch between 11.5 and 11.7 miles from the junction. After driving 14.8 miles from the junction at the end of the pavement (31 miles from US 89), you reach the aforementioned spur road leading to the trailhead, just before Skutumpah Road crosses Lick Wash.

The Hike

Begin the hike from the end of the spur road by walking down the rock-strewn wash. Bluffs of Navajo Sandstone, studded with ponderosa pines, rise ahead, and the wash seems to disappear between them. Soon you enter the sandstone-enveloped gorge, which quickly slots up, and you make your way ahead through the narrow slickrock corridor. Within minutes you reach a short fence that spans the gap between the canyon walls. Climb over or crawl through the fence, passing the only obstacle in the canyon.

After about 1 mile you leave the narrow passages behind and the canyon begins to open up, cutting through deep alluvial deposits that form benches flanking the wash, hosting a variety of shrubs and gnarled woodland trees. The canyon walls grow higher as you proceed, with smooth convex slopes of slickrock sweeping upward for hundreds of feet to the square-edged mesas above. Curved lines of cross-bedding on the slickrock shoulders reach to the base of fluted cliffs, decorated with dark black streaks and a brown patina of desert varnish. Ponderosa pines grow tall and straight at the base of the great cliffs and fringe the rims of the mesas above.

During the lower 2 miles of Lick Wash, you'll find cow trails to follow, shortcutting the minor meanders of the wash via the benches above. After about 3 miles, the hulking mass of No Mans Mesa fills your view ahead. By now the arroyo of Lick Wash has grown deeper. As you approach the mouth of the wash, you'll spy a shallow but obvious alcove on the left (north) canyon wall, scooped out of a shoulder of slickrock that projects into the canyon. This is your indication that it is time to leave the arroyo, which you should do before you come abreast of the alcove.

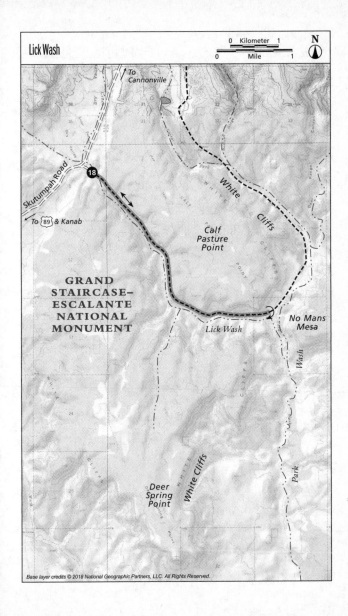

0   Kilometer   1

0   Mile   1

N

To Cannonville

Skutumpah Road

18

To 89 & Kanab

White Cliffs

Calf Pasture Point

CALF   POINT

WHITE   CLIFFS

GRAND
STAIRCASE-
ESCALANTE
NATIONAL
MONUMENT

Lick Wash

No Mans Mesa

Wash

CLIFFS

WHITE   Cliffs

Deer
Spring
Point

Park

Ascend out of the arroyo via cow trails to the north-side bench, where you will find an old 4WD track. Follow this faint doubletrack out into the valley of Park Wash, first east, then north, crossing a bench thick with the growth of big sagebrush and exotic Russian thistle (tumbleweed).

Calf Pasture Point and its sheer white cliffs loom 800 feet overhead on your left, while the equally impressive cliffs bounding No Mans Mesa define the eastern margin of the valley. These are the White Cliffs of the Grand Staircase, and they form the second tallest riser (only the Vermilion Cliffs are higher) in the series of cliffs and terraces that stair-step north out of the Arizona Strip into south-central Utah.

After enjoying the dramatic landscape of the White Cliffs, return the way you came.

Miles and Directions

0.0 From the trailhead, follow the wash southeast.

0.9 Passage widens and vegetation becomes more abundant.

3.1 View No Mans Mesa.

4.0 Reach Park Wash. Turn around and retrace your route.

8.0 Arrive back at the trailhead.

19 Wire Pass to Buckskin Gulch

Buckskin Gulch is the ultimate in canyon–country slot canyons. For 12.5 miles the gulch is enveloped in a very narrow gorge 100 to 200 feet deep, flanked by vaulting, convoluted walls of Navajo Sandstone. Buckskin Gulch is renowned not only because of its continuous, challenging narrows, but also because there is no other canyon like it in the world. Wire Pass, a gorge carved through The Cockscomb by Coyote Wash, is the most popular entry route into Buckskin Gulch. Wire Pass is short, but its narrows are even more confined than those in Buckskin. This is an excellent easy hike through Wire Pass into the famous gorge of Buckskin Gulch. You can extend the day hike as far as you wish by exploring Buckskin's narrows either upcanyon or down.

Distance: 3.4 miles round-trip
Hiking time: 1.5-2 hours
Difficulty: Easy
Trail surface: Wash route
Best season: Apr through early June; Sept through Oct
Canine compatibility: Dogs permitted, though navigating boulder jam with dogs can be difficult.
Water availability: Bring your own.
Hazards: Flash flood danger

Permits: Reservations for permits for overnight use required; day hikers must pay the appropriate fee at the trailhead register/self-service fee station. No fees required for children 12 and under.
Maps: USGS Pine Hollow Canyon (Utah-Arizona); BLM Paria Canyon–Vermilion Cliffs Wilderness; Hiker's Guide to Paria Canyon, or Kanab

Finding the trailhead: Follow US 89 to an unsigned, south-bound dirt road that branches off the highway at the west end of a

50-mph right-angle curve just west of The Cockscomb. Find the turnoff 0.8 mile west of milepost 25 and 34 miles northwest of Page, Arizona, or 0.2 mile south of milepost 26 and 37.5 miles east of Kanab, Utah.

While 4WD is recommended, this dirt road (known as House Rock Valley Road) is passable to 2WD vehicles in dry weather, barring severe runoff damage, and steadily ascends for 2.5 miles to a saddle separating The Cockscomb and Buckskin Mountain. Ignore the right fork to Fivemile Mountain at the saddle, then descend to a crossing of the Buckskin Gulch wash after 4.4 miles, where the road is subject to flood damage. The signed turnoff to Buckskin Gulch trailhead (located 0.2 mile east of the road), which you avoid, is located a short distance south of the wash.

You reach the spacious Wire Pass trailhead, located on the west side of the road, 8.4 miles south of US 89. Several undeveloped camping areas can be found en route to the trailhead. Pit toilets are in place at both the Buckskin Gulch and Wire Pass trailheads.

The Hike

As with any slot canyon, do not enter Wire Pass or Buckskin Gulch if there is the slightest chance of rainfall. In these canyons, as little as a quarter inch of rain can run off the slickrock landscape and turn the slots into inescapable death traps. Save this memorable trip for fair weather only.

From the Wire Pass trailhead, cross the road and follow the well-worn trail to the trailhead register and fee station. The trail ahead is well signed and sandy as it leads to a hiker's maze in a fenceline. The maze is a V-shaped passage that allows people, but not cows, to enter Wire Pass. Here Coyote Wash carves the portal to Wire Pass through The Cockscomb, where tilted red-tinted beds of Navajo Sandstone flank the wash.

Beyond the hiker's maze, signs direct you into the wash, a wide, sandy, and cobble-strewn avenue where the walking is easy and there are few obstacles to slow you down. Be aware, however, that hiking conditions can change with the passage of each flash flood. Always check current hiking conditions at the Paria Contact Station on US 89 before entering the canyon.

As you proceed, you gain views of the serrated crest of the Coyote Buttes rising to the south; ahead, the massive Navajo Sandstone cliffs of The Dive, where gaping alcoves have been scooped out of the walls, dominate the view. Benches flank the broad wash and support a scattering of junipers, sand sagebrush, Mormon tea, and squawbush. Rabbitbrush fringes the wash banks, sharing space with Apache plume, recognizable by its myriad white, roselike blooms and feathery fruits.

After following the wash for 0.8 mile, you reach the spur trail on the right (south) signed for Coyote Buttes. This trail will take you to The Wave, a beautiful and unusual sandstone rock formation, which is a popular destination for many hikers and photographers. Anyone interested in visiting the Coyote Buttes area will need a special permit in advance; contact the Grand Staircase–Escalante National Monument, Kanab Headquarters, for more information on permits. Continue on the main trail, bearing toward the left, to reach Wire Pass.

Wire Pass remains wide and shallow for 1.2 miles, bounded by low slickrock bluffs and sandy slopes. The slopes north of the wash are mantled in a veneer of white rocks and cobbles of the Kaibab limestone washed down over the ages from the slopes of the broad Buckskin Mountain to the west.

Eventually slickrock walls close in and the wash becomes rock-strewn. Soon thereafter, at 1.2 miles, you enter the first short stretch of narrows. Beyond the confines of this constriction, you are soon swallowed up in another very narrow slot where only 4 feet separate the canyon walls. Logs wedged between the tight, convoluted cliffs overhead are mute reminders of the tremendous force of flash floods in narrow desert canyons.

The third narrows are the deepest and most confining of all, pinching down to merely 2 feet wide in places. After exiting this final slot, you skirt a deep and shadowed alcove, then emerge into the boulder-littered wash of Buckskin Gulch. Downcanyon the walls quickly close in and Buckskin slots up. Though not as tight as Wire Pass, the gulch is still very

narrow and stays that way for many miles ahead. Interesting narrows are located upcanyon as well.

When you've had enough of being swallowed up deep within this confined gorge, backtrack to more open country and the trailhead.

Miles and Directions

0.0 From the Wire Pass trailhead, cross the road and follow the well-worn trail to the trailhead register and fee station.

0.8 Reach a spur trail on the right for Coyote Buttes; continue on the main trail, which bears toward the left, down the wash.

1.2 Narrows begin.

1.7 Reach the confluence with Buckskin Gulch. Turn around and return by the same route.

3.4 Arrive back at the trailhead.

20 Middle Route Trailhead to Cobra Arch

The hike to the aptly named Cobra Arch is a rewarding day trip for hikers with good route–finding ability. The route follows the rim of The Dive, high above the nearly invisible slot of Buckskin Gulch. Vistas en route are part of this trip's attraction, stretching across the vast, sandy surface of the Paria Plateau, punctuated by such slickrock landmarks as the Coyote Buttes, Steamboat Rock, and Wolf Knolls. True to its name, Cobra Arch is reminiscent of an ancient stone sculpture of a serpent's head.

Distance: 6.6 miles, round-trip

Hiking time: 4–5 hours, round-trip

Difficulty: Moderate, occasional Class 2 scrambling

Trail surface: Cross-country route; good route-finding ability required

Best seasons: Mid-Mar through May; Sept through Oct

Canine compatibility: Dogs permitted

Water availability: None available; bring your own.

Hazards: Exposure to steep drop-offs; inexperienced hikers risk becoming disoriented or lost

Permits: Not required

Maps: *West Clark Bench (Utah-Arizona) USGS quad; BLM: Paria Canyon–Vermilion Cliffs Wilderness map, or Smoky Mountain*

Finding the trailhead: The unsigned Long Canyon Road leading to West Clark Bench, branching south from US 89, is the first southbound road you reach 0.2 mile west of the Paria River Bridge, between mileposts 21 and 22. Find the turnoff 0.6 mile west of the turnoff to the Paria Contact Station, 30 miles northwest of Page, Arizona, or 42 miles east of Kanab, Utah.

After finding the turnoff, proceed south on Long Canyon Road. Due to deep sand, minimal maintenance, and possible flood damage, a 4WD vehicle is recommended and may be required to reach the trailhead. Do not attempt to drive to the trailhead in a low-clearance car. This road is a public road through private property for 0.9 mile. Shortly after leaving the highway, you pass the landmark teepees of the Paria River Guest Ranch and reach the first of five cattle guards after 0.25 mile. After passing over the fourth cattle guard, you enter public lands and soon thereafter reach the first sandy crossing of Long Canyon Wash, which is subject to washouts, 1.1 miles from the highway.

The road ahead, which can be slippery if not impassable when wet, ascends the shallow drainage of Long Canyon. You pass over the fifth and final cattle guard after 2.5 miles and cross the wash one last time at 3.1 miles. After the road tops out on the broad, sandy plateau of West Clark Bench at 4.2 miles, you pass the first of several right-branching roads, and you bear left at all but one junction ahead. This point is generally the end of maintenance on this road, so expect challenging driving conditions ahead.

As you continue along the sandy track, bear right at 5.1 miles, where a faint track branches left (north). After 7.8 miles, you reach a green steel gate. Park next to the large solitary juniper just beyond the gate or in one of the pullouts, where you can also camp, about 0.1 mile west of the gate.

The Hike

Only hikers entering the canyons of the Paria Canyon–Vermilion Cliffs Wilderness are required to obtain a permit and pay a fee. Hikers en route to Cobra Arch are not only able to enjoy a fee-free hike, they also enjoy the freedom of open spaces far above the shadowed confines of the narrow canyons.

Avoid this shadeless hike during the summer heat from about mid-May through mid-September, and be sure to carry plenty of water. The USGS West Clark Bench quad is highly recommended.

From the gate at the trailhead, follow a sandy old 4WD doubletrack south along the fence line. You rise gradually at first, then descend past the posted wilderness boundary to the juniper-studded rim of The Dive, 0.2 mile from the trailhead. Buckskin Gulch lies far below, but its narrow gorge is hidden from view by its tight canyon walls. Prominent features on the sandy tree-studded Paria Plateau to the south include the red slickrock butte of Steamboat Rock and the craggy Coyote Buttes to the southwest.

Now on a firm tread of slickrock at the rim, follow the rim east around the head of the first drainage, then south out to Point 5047. The walking is easier closer to the sandstone rim rather than along the sandy mesa top. As you proceed, views open to the northwest and north, reaching to the pyramid of Mollies Nipple and to the distant Pink Cliffs of the Aquarius Plateau.

When you reach Point 5047, you have a much better view of the gash of Buckskin Gulch. Your route ahead also comes into focus. The west-facing Navajo cliffs bounding Point 5119 are clearly visible about a mile away to the southeast. Your route will follow the sandy bench below, leading south along the base of those cliffs to the 4,800-foot flat beneath Point 5119. To get there, continue along the rim, heading east from Point 5047, enjoying expansive vistas along the way. Junipers dot the mesa of West Clark Bench, sharing space with wavy-leaf, or Harriman, oaks, a kind of scrub oak common in sandy locations, and Mormon tea, snakeweed, and the silvery mounds of roundleaf buffaloberry.

Pay attention to where the rim begins to curve southeast, at the head of a drainage. About 100 yards beyond the bend from east to southeast, there is but one break in the Carmel Sandstone on the rim. A solitary twisted juniper lies just below the break. Descend off the rim here over the crumbly sandstone, then mount the red Page Sandstone, where you find a 3-foot ledge. Just below the ledge you reach the Navajo Sandstone in the headwaters draw of the drainage and descend a 30-foot slickrock friction pitch down a shallow chute. Pause along the way and memorize your descent route so that you can easily find it upon returning.

The route ahead leads generally south across the sandy bench, and you work your way in and out of numerous small washes that dissect the bench. The route traverses deep, soft sand for 1 mile, but if you hug the base of the cliffs as best you can, you'll be walking on slickrock part of the time.

There is no avoiding the last, and steepest, sand hill, as you round the point and mount the 4,800-foot flat beneath Point 5119. When you reach the flat, which would make an excellent place to camp for backpackers who don't mind carrying water, follow along the foot of the Navajo Sandstone cliff, its cross-bedded slickrock stained a salmon hue by the overlying red beds of the Page Sandstone. Head southeast along the cliffs into a developing draw. About 0.2 mile down this draw, you'll see a mass of low, red slickrock domes off to your right (south). When you reach a low pour-off in the draw, turn south, descending several short slickrock friction pitches among the domes, heading for the presently visible arch at the southeast end of the dome complex.

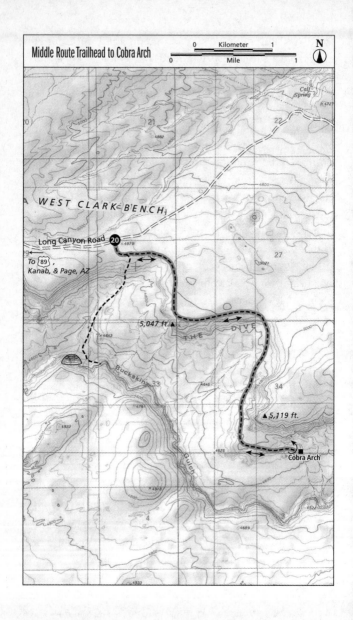

0   Kilometer   1

0   Mile   1

N

WEST CLARK BENCH

Long Canyon Road **20**

To **89**,
Kanab, & Page, AZ

5,047 ft. ▲

THE DIVE

Buckskin

Gulch

▲ 5,119 ft.

Cobra Arch

Calf
Spring

The arch is small but unique, a graceful ribbon of stone that is wide and flat at the top of the span, resembling the hood of a cobra's head. Indentations on either side are the "eyes" of the serpent.

After enjoying this very remote and unusual arch, carefully retrace your route to the trailhead.

Miles and Directions

0.0 Begin hiking from Middle Route Trailhead.

0.2 Reach the rim of The Dive.

1.9 Descend from the rim of The Dive.

3.3 Reach Cobra Arch. Turn around and return by the same route.

6.6 Arrive back at the trailhead.

About the Authors

Ron Adkison was an avid hiker and backpacker who began his outdoor explorations at age 6. Over more than thirty years of hiking, he logged more than 12,000 trail miles in ten Western states. He walked every trail in this guide to provide accurate, firsthand information about both the trails and features of ecological and historical interest.

Ron passed away in September 2009, but his love and enthusiasm for wild places live on in his sixteen guidebooks.

JD Tanner grew up playing and exploring in the hills of southern Illinois. He has earned a degree in Outdoor Recreation from Southeast Missouri State University and an advanced degree in Outdoor Recreation from Southern Illinois University in Carbondale. He has traveled extensively throughout the United States and is the director at Touch of Nature Environmental Center at Southern Illinois University in Carbondale.

Emily Ressler-Tanner grew up splitting time between southeastern Missouri and southeastern Idaho. She spent her early years fishing, hiking, and camping with her family. In college Emily enjoyed trying out many new outdoor activities and eventually graduated from Southern Illinois University with an advanced degree in Recreation Resource Administration. Emily instructs in the Outdoor Recreation Department at Southern Illinois University in Carbondale and is the executive director for the Friends of the Shawnee National Forest.

Together they have climbed, hiked, paddled, and camped their way across the United States. They co-instructed college-level outdoor recreation courses for several years before joining the staff at the Leave No Trace Center for Outdoor Ethics as Traveling Trainers. They currently reside in Southern Illinois.